About the Author

For over three decades, Simon has been working with children and young people in education and drum circle settings. This has enabled him to fine tune his creative, technical and interpersonal skills in search of meaningful developmental outcomes for his players.

In *Lion, Octopus, Panda, Duck,* he offers his unique insight into setting up and running social communication groups for players with additional needs or alternative learning styles, using rhythm activities.

In addition, his writing is infused with anecdotal stories and paradigms that capture the imagination and will connect with all who work in the field of rhythm and communication.

Lion, Octopus, Panda, Duck

A Training Manual:

Setting up and working with rhythm
to enhance social communication

For groups with additional needs and
alternative learning styles

Simon Stokes

First published by Talking Rhythms 2021
© 2021 Simon Stokes

ISBN: 978-1-9196478-0-7

Cover design and typesetting: Fuzzy Flamingo
www.fuzzyflamingo.co.uk

Lion, Octopus, Panda, Duck is dedicated to all the players, young people and staff who have been with me on this journey of discovery, sharing their energy, joining in the fun and generally being themselves in all their glory!

You have constantly kept me up to speed and driven my own personal development, helping to keep our times together meaningful and valued. Without you, this book would have no purpose.

Contents

Peer Reviews

The vibration of a drum permeates the bodies, hearts and minds of the people nearby.

Its sonic resonance massages and helps release the emotional, physical and mental tensions we carry in our life. Playing a drum goes beyond 'just making joyful noise'. It connects deeply within a person on a physical, emotional or spiritual level. When a caregiver facilitator introduces an interactive rhythm-based activity to a population of participants with additional needs and alternative learning styles, profoundly positive changes appear in their physiological and psychological states of being.

This book is not just a "How To" manual. Simon shares with us his extensive depth of experience working with groups with additional needs, and the profound positive interventions that lie behind the simple but powerful rhythm games he presents. In this book he provides a solid and workable framework on which to develop and deliver an effective program to the young people that you serve.

Accessibility, simplicity and fun is the key to this manual. Simon carefully lays out protocols, paradigms, fundamental guidelines and usable activities in an easy to follow and understandable sequence. His activity cards are easy to follow and understand, highly malleable, and can be mixed and matched to meet many types of classroom needs.

With Simon's guidance through this easy to follow manual, you don't have to be a musician or a drummer to successfully facilitate these rhythm games. All you have to do is care.

"Share your Spirit" in all the good works that you do. Through his book, Simon helps you do just that with rhythm-based activities.

Arthur E. Hull,
Head Elf of Village Music Circles

Lion, Octopus, Panda, Duck is a refreshingly simple, accessible and easy to read manual. The book focuses specifically on running social communication groups for players with additional needs, however the strategies discussed could be applied to any learning situation with any group of learners.

Simon draws on a wealth of knowledge and experience to give a detailed guidance on running these sessions both from a musical and a very practical perspective, helping non-music specialists, like myself, to feel confident in running similar sessions. The benefits of drumming are clearly explained and Simon's passion and enthusiasm for the subject is evident.

Mrs Cathryn Shilling
Head of School, Brocks Hill Primary School

This is an inspiring, wise and generous book. Inspiring because it is full of tested ideas and wonderful stories about the impact of Simon's work. Wise because Simon sets out the importance of self reflection on practice and the practitioner being led by the pupils. And generous because one could take this book and begin a programme immediately. Having seen Simon at work in our school where many of the students mentioned are based, I can attest to the power of this work in building social skills, creativity and attention. Perhaps even more importantly his work causes great joy. I cannot recommend this book highly enough.

Ingrid Spencer
Deputy Head, Oaklands School, Leicester

This manual is very informative and easy to read. I loved the anecdotal evidence!

It is clear that Simon speaks from a wealth of experience with working with children with SEND (special educational needs and disability) developing both social and communication skills alongside teaching drumming. For a non-musical person it seemed very clear and well structured so that others could follow the advice contained here and set up their own groups. As we go forward and mental health becomes more of a priority in schools, I would see a greater need for interventions including the use of music to develop and support well-being.

Mrs Nadine Curran
SEND Co-ordinator, Brocks Hill Primary School

This book will be a gift to those wishing to expand their rhythm skills and workshop practice into working with children with additional support needs. Here, Simon has very clearly shared his learnings from years of experience in these settings, and his intimate knowledge of the groups he has worked with shines through. There are plenty of activities for those seeking ideas – coupled with a solid grounding and well-presented frameworks for activity.

The clarity and sincerity of his writing makes it a perfect entry point for non-specialists on either side. Musicians who may wish to work in these settings will find helpful advice and insight from a practitioner's eye view, while staff members who may want to explore music-making with groups of children will find a wealth of entry points and activities that don't require you to be a musical specialist before trying them! An engaging, helpful, and accessible resource – I wish this book had been around when I started out!

Dr. Jane Bentley
Music in healthcare specialist and drum circle facilitation trainer, Art Beat, Scotland

Lion, Octopus, Panda, Duck – where did it come from?

It all started with a teaching career in Primary Education, including 15 years based in a learning support unit in a mainstream primary school. Here, I developed a love of supporting learners who needed to find unique and individual ways to learn. Starting my own company in 2007, Talking Rhythms, gave me the chance to combine this experience with a passion for music.

In the years since, I have delivered drum and music workshops to many areas of the community, from groups of two or three to events of 100 or more. However, one aspect of delivery has been consistent in pushing me to keep developing my style, knowledge and techniques: the sessions with small groups of children or adults with additional needs.

The physical, emotional and social challenges that these groups face in their day-to-day lives require great flexibility from the facilitator. The ability to constantly adapt equipment, resources and approaches in order to gain the most meaningful access to activities is essential.

This might mean having access to a drum that will stand at the footplate of a wheelchair, or a selection of beaters with adapted handles. It could mean being prepared to work in subdued lighting to reduce sensory input, or being doggedly consistent with the beginning and end of each session to provide consistent boundaries.

All of this having been said, when delivery is best matched to needs, we are provided with a fantastic opportunity to connect, to develop skills and language, and to rehearse social interactions.

The original intention in writing *Lion, Octopus, Panda, Duck* was simply to bring together years of practice and experience with this client group into one place for ease of access. However, in the process of writing, clear protocols and paradigms have emerged that have underpinned my approach and the work done in these sessions. This brings us to the manual you see before you, which I hope will offer clear, fundamental guidelines of planning and ethos along with practical, usable activities.

CHAPTER 1

This Manual: Origins and Some Basic Principles

Who is it for?

This manual is designed to support practitioners working with small groups of young pupils with a variety of additional needs. Much of the work that informs what you find here was undertaken in a Local Authority Special School in Leicestershire, with a significant number of pupils with needs on the autistic spectrum. That being said, many of the activities will lend themselves very easily to use with many other groups, with or without additional needs.

Why drum?

My main tool for these sessions is West African djembe-style hand drums, but that's not to say that the basic principles couldn't be delivered with a whole variety of percussion, or even homemade instruments.

Drumming itself has been part of our world culture since time immemorial. From the drumming of indigenous people and the journeying of shamans to the driving rhythms of the rock band, the use of rhythm to drive, motivate, unify and even heal has been universal. Arthur Hull, of Village Music Churches, who has inspired an international community of drum circle facilitators through his renowned facilitation play shops, says in his book *Drum Circle Facilitation*:

> "When people come together and drum, they are a fully interacting group, creating and sharing a rhythmical and musical experience."

As Arthur outlines in his book, the drum is a beautiful tool for asking questions, for providing a safe space to speak and be heard. The drum also allows us to practise using our voice and learn to give others the space to do the same.

On another level, drumming can also offer a platform to practise basic motor skills (left and right), fine motor control (hand positions and co-ordinated rhythms) and develop levels of concentration and cognitive understanding, alongside social communication. All of this and more is accessible within the activities contained here.

Benefits of drumming:

- Gives a safe space to speak and be heard.
- Lets players ask questions.
- Gives players a voice.
- Helps players learn to give others space.
- Practise gross motor skills.
- Develop fine motor skills – hand positions and control.

- Concentration – learning and relearning patterns of information.
- Cognitive development – reinforcing language and communication, building motor skills and social interaction.

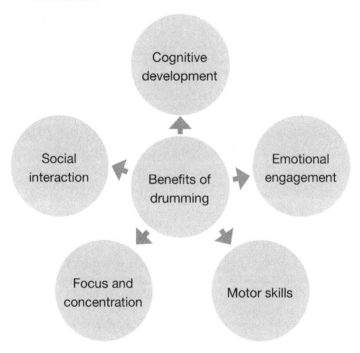

Why *Lion, Octopus, Panda, Duck*?

For many years, I have been accompanied on my travels by an old black kit bag stuffed to the brim with cuddly toys. These guys form the basis of many of my activities, sitting on the basic principle of:

'If you can say it, you can play it!'

They work individually to form:

- Rhythm loops:
  "Tiger, tiger, tiger…"

- Rhythm phrases:
  "Monkey, monkey, oo oo ah ah…"

- Or together to form rhythm sentences:
  "Lion – Octopus – Panda – Duck"

These rhythm loops, phrases and sentences even have a role to play in musical composition and hand placement – anyone who has been in one of these sessions will know them well!

Although rhythm loops and rhythm sentences might seem very similar, there is a key diagnostic and developmental element to these activities, which we will return to in the programme section.

Lion, Octopus, Panda, Duck: How it works

This manual outlines the approaches and techniques that are used in delivering these sessions. The following chapters contain an outline of the rationale and protocols that underpin the programme, along with practical examples of activities and links to the areas of development they are designed to support.

It is in no way intended that this will be a definitive article on this work; in fact, the very nature of the client group means that activities and delivery will need to be constantly tweaked and modified to meet the needs of the individuals and groups that you have before you. So, please feel free to develop and adapt as required. However, you will find a solid pack of foundational activities from which to lay out an effective programme.

Find your way around

Following on from Chapter 1 here, which outlines the origins of the manual and some of the protocols behind it, there are three further chapters, each detailing an aspect of the delivery and programme development, and an appendix with practical resources.

Chapter 2 – Getting Started: Before the Drumming Begins

This chapter covers some of the basics of setting up, equipment choices and environmental factors that need to be considered before the drumming starts.

Chapter 3 – Read the Signs

Here, we deal with establishing and managing some of the key skills designed to bring into focus some of the elements – emotional and psychological – of group dynamics that work together to maintain a responsive, needs-based setting.

Chapter 4 – Programme Development

This chapter focuses on the basics of developing a structured and progressive but flexible programme. In it, we examine the elements that can be mixed and matched to meet the working environment and needs of the group.

Appendix: – Activity Cards

Concluding with a practical resource, here you will find a series of practical activity cards designed to support a basic programme. Also contained here is an overview of the format of the activity cards with links to programme elements and development strands.

Alive and Well: Beyond 'Just Making Noise'

The rhythm of the drum is indeed something that is alive. It has the power to capture imaginations and unite people who have never met before, or who struggle with conventional forms of communication. However, it goes much deeper than this.

There are times when the playing of the drum goes beyond 'just making noise' and connects deeply within a person on a physical, emotional or spiritual level. Significant research has been done into the area of sound and music therapy. *Music Medicine* by Christine Stevens (2012) provides a good holistic introduction. She writes:

"From the simple act of walking to the creative beauty of dance, rhythm speaks to our bodies and expresses our innate groove. It is a deep biological, neurological pathway that we can access for healing, growth and development."

The combination of kinaesthetic and mental activity involved in rhythm-making offers itself as a perfect medium for generating personal health and development in line with the current focus on well-being and mindfulness. The act of being in a group and playing quite literally 'in time' with one another means that players are uniquely here within this moment, which allows for future-based anxieties or task-based targets to fall away.

This has been confirmed for me on more than one occasion by comments from players regarding their sense of well-being after leaving after a session, whether as a simple statement like 'I love drumming' or 'I could feel the drums right here in my chest', or a more complex social connection with other players. Time and time again, people's change in energy and the positive feelings they have when they leave the sessions are a testament to the power of the drums.

A Moment in Time: Examples

I wanted to share four moments when I have been powerfully reminded that this is more than just noise-making. These are responses that have spontaneously shown up to be unexpectedly powerful and significant, not only for the individual involved, but also for the group.

NB – All names have been changed, but stories are genuine.

In these four stories, we meet Jack (known to me as Smiler because of his responses), Iyad and Zac, and receive an apology from a lady who couldn't play. I have chosen them from different areas of my community and have added short examples of reflective learning to show how each example had an impact on my own learning and development.

1. Smiler: "Suddenly, I'm here"

Our first story illustrates the power of social connection through sound.

This session takes place in a whole-class group of Year 3 children, within a mainstream primary school, one of whom is significantly visually impaired and is supported by a learning assistant.

During the session, we have been working on a 'Rumble' activity (creating a rumble sound by players playing as fast as they can on their drums). Here, a member of the class comes to the centre of the circle and, by raising and lowering their arms, facilitates the whole group to play as fast as they can, loud or quiet, stopping and starting in response to the signals.

Smiler comes to the middle of the circle with his teaching assistant whispering instructions in his ear. All is quiet. Slowly, he raises his arms from his side and, as one, his classmates begin to play, getting louder as his arms raise, and quieter as he puts them down. Suddenly, he is smiling as he realises that everyone is listening to and watching him – he is in control! It's a rare moment that he gets this much upfront feedback and he loves it!

Reflective Learning

Social and emotional connection through sound.

Familiarity breeds desensitisation:

> It is very easy if you have been a frequent visitor to the centre of a drum circle to become desensitised to the effect that standing on this spot can have. It can be an intensely frightening or powerful experience. For some, to stand there knowing everyone is looking at them will be their worst nightmare; for others, having everyone's attention is delightful. Somewhere between the two, there is room for quiet encouragement to receive support from your peers, and a chance to learn the responsibility of being in control.

Lead with the 'door' open:

> On this occasion, it was Smiler's learning assistant who spotted the opportunity and suggested that they come to the centre. She knew him well and knew that this was on the edge of his confidence, but with enough potential for success to be worth trying. When working with one-off groups or groups that change frequently, it is a useful tip to leave the door open for the initiative of others, particularly if they know the players well.

Significance is palpable:

Sometimes, significant things happen that are only noticed by the individual concerned.

On this occasion, it was clear from the reactions of the other children that they were aware that this event was significant. A buzz went around the circle as they responded dynamically to the rumble commands – they were aware of the significance of the moment and revelled in it.

2. "I'm sorry I didn't play"

Being aware of the vibrational impact of drumming.

This time, the person is with a group of staff from a local GP practice. We are looking at the concept of 'pulse' and how important it is to the rhythm of our lives. Musically with the drums, the pulse is the main beat of the music and determines the tempo of the music, but it also provides the anchor for the rhythms that we play. It allows us to be unique and yet respond as a group, and to add individual contributions to the whole.

In our daily lives, there is a pulse too – it can be felt in the patterns and activities of each of our days. Here, the pulse rate will change depending on how many tasks we have to do, how much time we have to do them and how important they are to us. Importantly, how much control we have over that pulse and rhythm has a significant impact on our well-being. This session was designed to explore the pulses of the workplace, who had control of them and how we could manage them effectively to maintain good health. (But that's another book!)

Out of nowhere at the end of the session, I was taught a completely different lesson. I had noticed one member of staff who was quite reluctant to join in the drumming, although she interacted fully in the conversation. She came to me at the end of the session and apologised.

"I'm sorry I didn't play," she said, "but it was hurting me." "That's okay," I said, pointing to the arthritis in my fingers, "I have trouble sometimes, too." Then she stunned me, "No, my hands are fine, it was the sound from the drums making me uncomfortable," and she gestured to her body.

This was my awakening to understand that the vibrational power of the drums was way more significant than I had ever previously realised. Everybody is reacting on some level to the physical vibrations coming from the sound of the drums. Obviously for most people, these sensations are positive, even if not consciously recognised by the participant.

There is a great deal of information available now from research into the vibrational qualities of sound, and opportunities for sound therapies and immersive experiences, such as gong 'baths', are readily available from a short online search.

It became clear, too, that this is a significant factor to take into account when working with clients with additional needs. I needed to take into consideration this vibrational level of interaction and the effect that it might have on individuals, particularly those with heightened sensory responses.

Reflective Learning

Subconscious responses to sound and vibration:

This is an important layer of awareness for leaders working in this medium and has a number of different layers to consider.

Increased sensitivity to sound:

Players might have an increased sensitivity to sound. Even sound levels that feel comfortable to some may cause others some discomfort, and if they have decreased or impaired communication skills then we have to rely on our visual radar to pick this up.

Proximity to harsh or loud sounds:

Some instruments are louder or have more percussive impact on the ears. Sitting next to a highly-tuned djembe drum or a tone block or a cow bell, for example, may produce transients (peaks) of sound that can cause discomfort. It is important to keep in mind that there are two major factors in hearing damage: loud, consistent noise over time, and sudden peaks of harsh sound, even of a very short duration.

Sensitivity to vibrations:

We are all subject to the vibrational impacts from sounds and a group of drums creates a significant impact. As we can see from this account, some individuals are far more highly attuned to these sensations. This may lead to negative complaints of headaches or feeling sick.

Conversely, on the positive side, it is one of the key factors in the creation of well-being and a significant feelgood factor. After all, rhythm has the ability to induce dancing in most people. It is important to take notice of these two indications.

Awareness of the first requires a duty of care for our clients, not to inflict uncomfortable or invasive sounds, and the second opens up opportunities to develop activities by adding movement to our sessions. This awareness is crucial to the success of a session and the comfort of players. (See Chapter 2 – Getting Started.)

3. Iyad: Bass-level eye contact

How being brave enough to act on impulse and do something different or unusual can sometimes lead to surprising results.

Iyad is a young adult, he is in a wheelchair and we have been drumming together in a group for a few weeks. His movements are often quite random and his feet are held onto his footplates with straps to avoid unintentional injuries to himself or others. Although he finds coordinating his hands difficult, he can manage, with help, to hit a drum on occasion, but he just loves the sound of everyone else drumming. He becomes more and more animated when we drum, to the point where sometimes the energy of his movements causes his chair to leave the floor! He smiles a lot but finds consistent eye contact difficult, so he is hard to read.

On this particular occasion, I was becoming concerned for him as we had been drumming for a while and he was quite animated. I decided to facilitate a slower groove that the others hooked onto and took on well. Iyad began to calm and his movements became less animated. On the spur of the moment, I decided to stand in front of him, holding my drum a short distance away from him so that the bass vibrations from the drum could be felt in his chest. The transformation was almost instant. Normally as we are drumming, in his excitement, Iyad's arms are out wide and his movements are very big and very strong, which causes his support worker to keep on his toes to avoid accidentally being struck. On this occasion, he slowly brought his arms in and wrapped them around his chest as he listened to and felt the drum. He looked up and gave direct eye contact, with a smile.

Staff working in the group were astonished at the change – and the speed with which it had taken place – and it prompted a discussion about ways in which music could be used in this way in the future.

Reflective Learning

Being aware of your surroundings and client sensibilities.

Maintaining the ability to be able to act spontaneously without causing discomfort or crossing personal or social boundaries.

There is a huge potential risk taken in this story. To suddenly stand in front of someone who is clearly very sensitive and reactive to sound and point a large drum at them has the potential to create an uncomfortable and possibly distressing overload of responses. However, there are a number of factors at play here:

- Previous experience and knowledge of the group.
- A sense of trust and fun built up over weeks.
- Good interactions with support workers, both with myself and clients.
- An established culture of trying new things.

The final and most important was that the sense from Iyad was always one of fun and excitement. Had these things not been in place then it would not have been appropriate to take the risk.

Brave enough to take the risk:

It's not clear to me even now what gave me the impulse to pick up my drum and try this. There was probably a cue from his reaction to the slower groove that the group was establishing, but there was also an intuitive element that can't be pinned down that prompted me to try it.

Paced and considered action:

Once the decision is made to act on an impulse then your radar must be switched on to the

maximum. It is a process of slowly feeling your way through the activity, constantly aware of any adverse reaction that might indicate discomfort or an undesired response. The risks are there, but as can be seen from Iyad's story, great rewards are possible too.

Know your boundaries and when to be risk-averse:

These spontaneous pathways can only be taken when you're clear of the boundaries for yourself and those you are working with. Some of these are consistent across the board, such as personal respect and safeguarding of individuals, and others will change depending on situations. Some groups will find it acceptable or even fun to challenge things, and will readily accept if they don't work. Others will find it threatening and stressful. Know yourself, know your group, don't be afraid to stand at the edge of what you know, and try something new when circumstances are right.

4. Zac's Owl

Leaving space for players to support each other.

Working with a small group of Year 4 primary children, we are using animal cards to create rhythms (something we'd

been doing for a couple of previous sessions). This week, the cards have musical notation under the animal words.

One young player, Zac, who is on the autistic spectrum, and sometimes has difficulty fitting in with the sessions, took particular pleasure in the process of saying "owl" over four beats, "owwwwwwllllllll," and it caused him great hilarity. On a previous occasion, this laughing had become uncontrolled and had made it difficult for him to continue with the group. However, on this occasion, the rest of the group had begun to join in with his long owl and before long, three of the girls had also added a body motion for the duration of the beat. Now, everyone was laughing and there was a great expectation for whenever the owl card would return to the top of the pack.

Reflective Learning

How leaving space for group ownership leads to enhancement of group objectives.

Leave the moment open:

> There is always a point at which choices are made about what will happen next. One response here, in light of previous experiences, could have been to 'shut down' the laughter to prevent loss of control by Zac – "No girls, it's not funny, let's count the owl beats." However, by leaving the moment open, space was left for the group to offer input.

In your own style:

> By seizing the moment and joining in with their own

actions, the girls honoured what Zac had offered to the group and added their own style, complementing and adding movements to his vocal interpretation.

Collective moments of unity:

Often in a group, there will be a common attachment to an event or a theme. By allowing the group to react and add to this spontaneously, moments of unity will arise. In this case, as individuals in the group responded and added their own style to the activity, other members of the group were encouraged to do the same. The laughter at the end was a sign of a collective understanding that we generated something that was fun and of value.

Peer-to-peer teaching:

By their actions, the group had offered Zac an alternative scenario for managing his laughter. Instead of finding himself laughing on his own, he found the group laughing with him. They also all managed and controlled the laughter as they took it in turns to join in. It was a useful lesson for Zac.

In this way, the original objectives for this session were superseded and the session took on a special quality beyond that for which it had originally been designed.

These are just a few examples of those moments that arrive unexpectedly and unplanned, but they serve to remind us that this is so much more than just drumming or noise-making, and that the opportunity for learning, development or community are always just around the corner.

Summary of Chapter 1

This chapter lays down some of the basic principles that underpin all of the work in this manual. They remind us to:

1. Use simple, accessible cues for rhythm generation.
2. Remember it's so much more than just noise.
3. Enjoy and inhabit sound and rhythm as a pathway to connection.
4. Be mindful of the power of the drum on all levels – visual, auditory, vibrational.
5. Stand at the edge of what we know and risk for reward.
6. Offer up ownership and be prepared to learn as we lead.

CHAPTER 2

Getting Started:
Before the Drumming Begins

Much of the work contained in *Lion, Octopus, Panda, Duck* has been inspired by a regular weekly session in a local special school. The session takes place over two hours and involves four groups of approximately 10 young people each morning. The sessions have been running for seven years now, and are some of the most challenging and rewarding times I have had with Talking Rhythms.

This chapter outlines a number of baseline protocols that will assist in establishing a safe, managed and productive environment for your rhythmical explorations, even before your first drum is struck.

Use Local Knowledge

The first session with any group is often, for the large part, a process of trial and error, going through which activities will work and which level will be needed to best suit the group and maintain interest and connection. However, any information that can be gleaned by talking with supporting staff beforehand, either prior to the session or even if necessary, just before the session, e.g. "I'm going to try this today, does this sound reasonable?" is enormously helpful in this process.

As with many things, the simple questions are often most helpful, e.g.:

> "Have they done anything like this before?"
> "How are we at following instructions?"
> "Is there anything in particular I should be aware of?"

Be prepared, also, to let people know what your expectations are in terms of running the group.

I will:

- Take charge and lead the session.
- Offer a variety of facilitated activities.
- Provide visual and auditory cues and instructions.
- Keep the session moving and manage behaviours at a group level.
- Ask you to take a lead on specific behaviour management patterns/strategies for individuals.

And don't forget to hold out the invitation:

> "Please don't be afraid to jump in if you think you need to, or if you can see an idea might run further for a particular player and you'd like to try."

These initial instructions will help to enhance your professional standing and shape the working relationships that will support much of your future work. Once these personal relationships are established, you can begin to set the foundations for your physical workspace, instruments and resources.

So, begin by taking a good account of the room or environment you are going to be working in. The following paragraphs offer some advice on how to get the best out of your room, kit, sound quality and resources.

Managing the Working Environment

The issue of health and safety is paramount, not only for your players but also for yourself. Ensuring that the working environment is physically safe is of course your number one priority, but it is also our responsibility to ensure the comfort and emotional safety of our players. It is rarely possible to find the perfect environment; however, there is usually a way to modify the room setup or group timetable to make the best of your environment. There will always be the rare occasion though where you need to be prepared to say, "I'm sorry, it won't work in here."

Taking Charge of Your Room

In his workshops, or "Playshops" as he refers to them, Arthur Hull states that one of the first priorities for any facilitator is to: "Take charge of your room."

If people are to engage, interact and learn or develop in any situation then some basic factors must be in place. The need to feel valued and safe is paramount. A well-organised, comfortable space that provides for the needs of the players is essential, more so in client groups where sensitivity to the immediate environment can be heightened. The initial list is a simple one. Do you have:

1. Enough space – to be comfortable and accommodate any additional needs, e.g. wheelchair or extra chairs for staff?
2. Enough suitable chairs – both for players and sizes of drums?
3. Appropriate lighting and heating?
4. An area free from distractions from outside sources?
5. A space that is conducive to manageable sound quality?

In schools and similar environments, space is at a premium and it will occasionally be that your usual room is unavailable. A change of room can be inconvenient for us, but it's important to be aware that the implications for a player whose concept of space is very different from ours can be significant. Going from a small room with a reasonably subdued sound quality to a large hall with booming echoes can create heightened anxiety or seriously ramp up energy levels. This can cause displays of exaggerated behaviours, such as an inability to stay seated, running around available space, or shouting and banging a drum in order to explore the new available sound space.

Every space will have its own features that help or hinder the success of a group session, but by careful (not necessarily lengthy) observation, we can maximise the former and minimise the latter. It is important to be aware that there are often more factors to consider when working in additional needs settings. Below is a personal example that demonstrates the range of factors that need particular consideration in an environment.

A Standard Tuesday

My aim is always for my groups to come into an environment that is set up and ready to play. On a Tuesday morning, I arrive early enough to allow for two things – firstly to set up the room, and then to run over the programme for each group to make sure the resources are at hand. Setting up the room includes a number of basic things, such as liaising with the premises officer to get 15 chairs delivered to the room (they are usually there before me now!), and making sure there are no resources from previous classes left to cause a distraction. This particular room always involves the repositioning of a large floor PE gym mat that would lend itself to rolling on and would be too great a temptation for some individuals in the groups. Unlocked cupboards also present temptation for some children, so it is worth checking that doors are secured. The same applies to fire doors and external exits.

On the subject of access, be mindful of the little things. I am always careful to shut the entry door behind me on accessing the room. The doors are all double handled (one high, one low), so as to prevent unassisted access. Whilst it is great that children walk down the corridor and look in or wave, if the door was left open, one or two would be tempted to come in and explore. Although there is never a problem with people wanting to see or play the drums, it should be remembered that we are working within a given context and a given set of establishment or community guidelines. However we feel personally about engaging with players, if we do not respect these community boundaries, we will not be asked back.

This simple 'open door' scenario illustrates the way we have to take these additional factors into consideration. If the door were to be left open, permitting unlimited access to the room and drums, then the following issues could arise if pupils entered the room independently:

- They are not where they are supposed or expected to be.

  In the school in this example, there is a programme of developing independence in pupils. One stage of this is increasing their ability to move around school independently, starting with making their way to the classroom in the morning. If they have ended up in my room then:
  - They are not where they are supposed to be.
  - The person expecting them doesn't know where they are.
- They have been distracted from their purpose.

  Memory function and the ability to self-organise are key issues for many pupils in this setting. By leaving my door open, I have provided an added distraction that may hinder them and prevent them from completing their directed task.
- Unknown quantity.

  There is also an individual, who is possibly unknown to you, in a room with lots of equipment and their reactions and responses may be unpredictable. They may just sit and stay at a drum, it may be fun to run around the circle and pull over all the drums because they make a nice sound as they hit the floor, or the drums may be ignored altogether in favour of climbing on the cupboard in the corner of the room. In any event, you now have a dilemma as to how to intervene in order to protect your equipment, the child, or both.

- You are on your own.

  In this scenario, it's not possible to leave the room because you can't now leave the student unattended, yet at the same time, you need another adult in order to stay on the right side of safeguarding protocol.

All this could simply be avoided by being aware of who has access and when. Safeguarding is not just about keeping others safe; it is also important to stay aware and avoid situations that put your own reputation or safety at risk.

It may seem a little extreme and negative to make these points in this way, and this is not to say that I don't on occasion open the door to a child looking for social contact or who wants a tap on a drum on the way to class. The point here is to be:

- Aware of potential risks.
- Aware of community guidelines and expectations.
- Aware of your role and responsibilities in this context.

Take charge of your room, even before you start. You decide how it looks and feels, how the space is to be used and who has access and when. Once you have established your environment then attention falls to consideration of your equipment and resources, and how best to use them.

Matching Kit for Purpose

There are two key components to matching kit successfully for any group of this nature: physicality and sound quality. All of the information below has been learned at the coal face of practical experience, some of it the hard way, so it's offered as basic ideas that may help to avoid some pitfalls, and to set a safe and effective base for your sessions.

- **Basic Setup**

This will obviously vary according to the size and needs of the group, along with the equipment available to you.

As you can see, the basic setup is djembe drums: 10 drums are brought in each week and the school provides any

additional drums needed. Whenever possible, staff are encouraged to be part of the group, too. This facilitates good interactions between staff and pupils, as well as providing good role models to follow. There are two further benefits; it provides a good solid core of sound for activities, and staff are able to benefit from the well-being attributes of drumming together.

Percussion instruments are introduced for certain groups (see sticks and handheld percussion on page 31) and are often used as a foundation for choice-making or turn-taking activities. Where interest levels and attention spans allow, it is also fun to showcase a different type of drum, bringing a cajon, bodhran talking drum, or tabla, for example. These are ideal catalysts for language development, talking about their sounds, shapes or designs and can open discussion about places of origin and culture.

So, this is what the basic setup for this group looks like. Let's take a moment to think about how the type of group we're working with might have an impact on this.

- **Physicality: Matching Drums to Players**

It is important for players to be comfortable with their instrument so that they can focus as much as possible on the core activities for the session. This means no one should be struggling to support their instrument and play it at the same time. With djembe drums, wherever possible, drums should sit at a comfortable height for both hands to reach with minimal effort.

In groups where additional factors are present, such as wheelchairs or limited manual dexterity, it is useful to have a variety of options available. It's also useful to have a tambor  or frame drum that can be handheld or put on a lap or wheelchair tray. Different styles of drums are beneficial, including some with a narrow base that can sit comfortably on the footplate of a wheelchair, larger drums with beaters that can be placed alongside a player's dominant hand for easy access, or smaller drums that can be held in front of the player by a helper for easy access.

It is possible to go to the lengths of providing drums on stands, which can be positioned at an appropriate angle for the range of movement of the player, but bear in mind this means more kit to carry and more time to set up. In these circumstances,  it is well worth having a selection of handheld percussion available for those who don't wish to drum, or for whom contact with the drum is difficult or uncomfortable.

In some cases, there will be players who, either because they are having a bad day or in reaction to something else that is happening in the group, will suddenly push their drum to the floor. (It is important to note that this may be an instinctive reaction rather than deliberate act.) This has a number of consequences. It is hazardous for the player or person sitting next to them, or may damage the drum itself. It requires an intervention to re-engage the player with the group, and with younger children, it can often lead to  a frustrating succession of copycat drum pushing, which can derail a whole session. Depending on the reason for this reaction in the first instance, a very simple solution is a drum belt, which hooks to one side of the drum around the player and back to the drum (detachable straps from shoulder bags work wonders). In many cases, this removes the impetus to push: because the drum cannot fall, there is no reason to push.

Remember, always consult support staff and explain to the player before offering belts, and make every effort to understand the background to the behaviour. For example, if the player is not enjoying the experience or the sound levels are driving them into overload but they do not have the language to make this known, then pushing their drum over may be their only way of letting you know. It may be necessary to employ other strategies to reduce their anxiety. Leaving the room for a short time may be beneficial, or sometimes reining in the other players (quieter or slower) or changing the activity might be enough. It might even be as simple as moving seats if the player is unsure of or feels threatened by the person next to them. Local knowledge of staff is vital in this situation. Don't be afraid to ask, "Is this a usual response?" or "Are we having a bad morning?" even "How about if we…?" as these can all lead to understanding and helpful solution responses.

- **Sticks and handheld percussion: know your group**

Many of the activities in this manual are easily replicated with handheld percussion or a mix of percussion and drums. I tend to gravitate towards hand drums for two reasons:

1. It gives instant kinaesthetic feedback to the player when playing: e.g. "right hand", "left hand", it can be felt in the hands.
2. It removes a layer of technicality that is added with sticks.

However, in some circumstances the use of a stick on percussion or a drum adds a range of accessibility to a player with low mobility or poor coordination. It may not be physically possible for the player to position their body to reach a drum, but a stick can allow the drum to be positioned in such a way as to make playing achievable.

A good investment is a small selection of sticks with enlarged or easy-grip handles. It is worth taking a moment before giving out any sticks to check whether there is any tendency to 'mouth' objects to avoid risk of choking. When giving out sticks, it's also worth considering the possibility that such objects may be thrown or used to strike out, either deliberately or as an involuntary action, potentially causing injury to others.

It is not the intention here to scare you into never using handheld percussion with these groups, but just to sound a note of caution to 'know your group' before you hand out percussion gear.

It's also helpful to get into the habit of a short, clear demonstration of how a particular instrument is expected to be played beforehand. Additionally, this gives a handy baseline to come back to if needed – "Remember how a tone block is played" – to bring a player back to an appropriate use of the instrument.

Whilst identifying and sorting kit, it's important to be aware of the sound quality of individual instruments and the ensemble as a whole.

•   **Sound Quality**

There are many factors to think about in terms of sound quality, although we are not looking for recording-quality sound here. In this context, we are looking for a communal sound experience where everyone is able to access the rhythm-making process. If players are going to be able to bring together simple rhythmic patterns, derived from verbal and visual cues (see activity cards) and blend them into a corporate rhythm, they are going to need to be able to hear both themselves and others. The key factor in enabling this is to manage volume levels.

We have already considered the effects of the environment on our sound – now putting that together with the sound quality from the chosen kit, we can begin to get an idea of the effect that these sound levels may have on our group and our ears.

There have been times when I have taken a particular group of instruments to an event only to set aside one of them (e.g. cowbells) because I just couldn't guarantee having enough control over the players to maintain appropriate sound levels in that particular room.

The following paragraphs offer three simple ways to manage volume using signals or cues, placement of the drums and a technique I have termed social engineering.

Volume control

- **Use a signal**

The simplest and yet most effective tool for the control of volume is to teach and consistently use a signal that indicates 'volume down'. This can be as simple as raising your arms out wide in front of you above head height and gradually lowering them until the required volume is achieved.

It is often all you need to do in order to lower stress levels for particular players, ensure safe levels of sound and bring a higher level of musicality to the groove, simply because players are able to hear each other better.

Author giving 'volume down' signal

If a simple signal is ineffective or only reduces sound levels for a short period before they rise again, then it is time to redirect activities. Change to a call and response activity where a leader plays a short pattern to be repeated by the group, immediately building in breaks to the continuous sound level. Alternatively, if the group is able, a game such as 'Hear that song' could be used, where a leader chooses two or three players to play their song to the group, thus giving the same immediate drop in volume levels.

• Drum positions – on or off the floor

This is a useful technique to use if your room is going to generate too much energy and you are unsure about volume control. Under normal circumstances, a djembe or hand drum would be positioned at an angle to allow space between the floor and the base of the drum for the sound to escape.

Standing the drums flat on the floor will immediately reduce their sonic impact. You could always start in this mode and then as control is established and you have more confidence in the group, the drums could be moved to a more traditional position. This has the added bonus of a 'wow moment' as players get to hear the full force of the bass from their drums for the first time.

In some groups, just the effort and dexterity to keep the base of the drums off the floor is too much. It is possible to run whole sessions with drums standing flat on the floor. One thing to be aware of here is that this can make the impact of hand on drum a little harder, so safe, gentle hand strokes need to be demonstrated and a constant eye kept for players who are playing their drums with excessive force.

If all else fails, going back to your knowledge of your kit and applying a little product placement – or what I term social engineering – can help a great deal.

• Social Engineering

This is a simple exercise of matching a player to a particular instrument. You will know which of your drums are the loudest or have the most impact on the room, and which of your players have the least control or the least amount of consideration for others in the group. Social engineering is simply a process of keeping these two factors separate from each other.

This will probably need some careful strategy, as from experience, they will be inextricably drawn to each other. So, allocating players with specific places as they come into the room, or playing a game that requires players to switch places

– and by default instruments – or any other subterfuge that achieves the same result, is helpful in this process.

Knowing your kit and gently guiding players to or away from specific drums will help to keep the balance of your group and manage your sound quality.

Manageable volume control is key for two reasons:

1. It allows players to hear each other, which immediately increases the musicality of any groove.
2. For the health and safety for both our players and ourselves – this works on an emotional level as well, as high-energy grooves can cause anxiety for some players.

- **Protect your hearing**

It is important to remember that whilst a group of players might come to you for a set time, you may well be going on to run further sessions, thus adding to your accumulated sound absorption time. If this is the case, it's well worth considering some good-quality ear protection.

If you want to find out more about this topic, there's plenty of information available online – here's a couple of helpful links to get you started.

- Health and Safety Executive:
  - https://www.cdc.gov/nceh/hearing_loss/what_noises_cause_hearing_loss.html
- Noise Exposure Limits:
  - https://www.noisehelp.com/noise-dose.html

In summary, we have gained four strategies to manage volume:

1. Volume down signal.
2. Redirect activities.
3. Place drums.
4. Social engineering.

Before we finish this section, it is worth a brief word on the management of visual aids and other resources during a session. A fuller description of types and uses of resources will come in Chapter 4 on Programme Development, but here are some brief ideas about preventing resources from derailing a session.

- **Timing is Everything**

Even with the greatest visual resource, if it is brought into a session at the wrong time, it will be a distraction rather than an aid. Have resources accessible so that you can manage how and when you want them to have an impact.

If it's visible, it's in the game:

Almost anything can look interesting, and that colourful card or the tail of a kangaroo left visible will be enough for someone to come from the other side of the room to take a look, regardless of what you are doing at the time. Have a simple storage system that keeps resources hidden until needed.

• Refocusing often involves negotiation

Once the kangaroo is out of the bag, so to speak, this item involves taking a diversion from your intended topic to use the resource, or risks a protracted discussion over getting the kangaroo back into the bag. It is important to balance the needs of the group with the individual's focus on the resource, and this plus your knowledge of the group, will determine the best strategy for maintaining the momentum of the session. See 'remembering your intention' on page 39.

• Personal means nothing

On a more serious note, it is important to be aware of any personal bags you may have with you and what they may contain. Remember that social convention means nothing to some of our players, and a bag is a bag and fair game if they want to have a look. This may lead to a little embarrassment on our part or a possibly dangerous situation if we have forgotten to remove our headache medication. Personal phones are also a major safeguarding issue and as part of their policies, many schools or establishments will ask you to leave your phone in the office if seen using it on site.

Each group and environment will bring with it its own challenges and hazards, and it is not the intention (nor would it be possible) to cover them all here. What is offered is a framework of awareness and preparation for setting up a group in these contexts.

In concluding this chapter, there is one more concept to share that goes right to the heart of our practice.

- **Take a moment to remember your intention**

Now that the room is set and your resources are to hand, it's important to take a moment to sit back and remember why you do this.

What is your intention?

- For each player.
- For each group.
- For yourself.

The concept of establishing, knowing and holding onto our intentions is a significant one. On the wall in my study, there is a small piece of paper, on which is printed a quote from Arthur Hull's book on drum circle facilitation. He quotes his friend and fellow facilitator, Sunray. It says:

> "I remind myself each time I facilitate not to be invested in my plan and to be heavily invested in my intention." – *Drum Circle Facilitation,* Arthur Hull, p. 80

The concept of being true to your intention has kept me focused and provided direction wherever and whenever I remember to use it. If my intention for this group is that they should be happy, comfortable, fully engaged and learning, then it matters not that Fred has decided to drag the kangaroo out of the bag way before I wanted to use it.

Let's use the kangaroo now, the group is still engaged, Fred is learning, the intention is still intact.

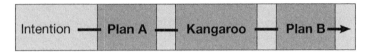

It's not always that easy and, sometimes, what Fred wants to do with the kangaroo just doesn't help your group or your session delivery. However, more often than not, understanding and holding your intentions will provide a clear route out of an impending crisis. Then sometimes, every now and again, it's also valuable and professional to say, "This isn't working, let's regroup next week and try again."

Getting Started Summary

So, there you are. You've set your room, brought the right kit, thought about your environment and your players (all of which is essentially your basic risk assessment process). You have established a good relationship with other adults and players in the room – now go and do your stuff!

1. Use local knowledge.
2. Be aware of your environment.
3. Take charge of your room.
4. Match kit for purpose.
5. Plan for sound quality and volume.
6. Employ social engineering if necessary.
7. Manage your resources.
8. Set your intentions.

CHAPTER 3

Read the Signs

One of the joyful features of this particular client group is that no two sessions are ever guaranteed to be the same; interactions, reactions and processes within the group are consistently subject to a whole raft of additional influences. Some of these may be external: "My bus was late this morning," "It's wet and windy outside and I haven't had a break yet," any of which can be significant if you are driven by routine or are particularly susceptible to environmental input. Alternatively, the influences may be coming from internal stimuli, which might be so subtle as to not even occur to the casual observer. Particularly for players on the autistic spectrum, triggers can be very individual (see Drivers, Triggers and Filters, p. 45). They might be centred on changes in the environment, particular sounds, noises, smells or changes in emotional status that can't be communicated. In these circumstances, local knowledge is invaluable. Speak to someone in regular contact who knows this individual well. Understanding and managing these physical and emotional responses is key to maintaining equilibrium with sessions.

Managing Emotions

It is useful to remember that we, too, carry around with us multiple experiences, reactions and responses that we use to interpret and function within the world. It is useful when we are faced with unexpected or unusual responses to take a step back, unhook our expectations and default reactions, and take a moment to remember our intentions and refocus our responses.

This distinction between reactions and responses is a simple but powerful tool to have in our repertoire. It only takes a moment to implement it, but can yield significant results when remembered.

React or Respond? A Scenario

It's a regular session. As a result of something that has happened in the room, a player has reacted aggressively and is now focusing that aggression on you. It's a natural process of our sympathetic nervous system under these circumstances to prepare our bodies for a fight or flight response.

Fight or flight:

> "The instinctive physiological response to a threatening situation, which readies one either to resist forcibly or to run away." – https://lexico.com/definition/fight_or_flight

Our energy will become heightened, along with a variety of physiological processes, such as increased heart rate, faster breathing and raised blood pressure. In this situation, it would be easy for us to 'react' rather than to 'respond'. A reaction is likely to come from our own fear of the aggressive outburst or annoyance at the disruption of the session, which may bring our energy up to match the level of the outburst. A response comes from that moment we take to remember our intentions and focus on the best outcome, rather than the current behaviour. This has the effect of bringing our energy level down, or at least allowing us to present a lower energy to the outside world.

- Reaction: high energy, large presence, possibly dominant or aggressive body language, "I need you to…"
- Response: lower energy, consistent presence, calm body language, "Let's see if we can…"

Responses will need to adapt to different players and situations, but the key is to come from a position of response rather than reaction. It doesn't have to be a long process to switch to response, just that moment to remember to step back. This helps to get 'me' out of the way and to 'hear' what verbal and non-verbal signals are being presented more clearly, which in turn allows a more effective response over time.

In order to be able to respond effectively in this way, it is essential to have as much information as possible at our fingertips. This is where our own radar function becomes most helpful.

Radar: Eyes, Ears and Gut Instinct

Having established that we are working with a living, breathing, dynamic entity, one principle that is going to ensure our success is our ability to connect to our players on both an individual and a group level. The process needed to collect the external information that drives this connection is what Arthur Hull refers to as our 'Radar Triplicity'. He says:

> "The three peripheral reading tools – vision, learning and feeling – function together as your radar to read your rhythm circle. A well-balanced radar gives you all the information you need to best serve the group you are facilitating." – *Drum Circle Facilitation*, Arthur Hull

> NB It's well worth investigating Arthur's concept of triplicities, as they are central to his work and great foundations to build on.

It is possible to get a good initial indication of how your group is going to start a session by noting the way they arrive at your door. Remembering to stay relaxed and visually scan the room will keep information coming to you. Being relaxed also means that your peripheral vision will be working more efficiently, meaning your whole field is covered. This is useful when someone decides to make a beeline for your nicely prepared resources ready to scatter them to the four corners of the room, or to bring your attention to the player who is sitting towards your side but no longer focused on their drum and needs to be re-engaged. It can even be helpful, on occasion, if a cuddly toy is being returned to you forcefully and unexpectedly and you have to duck!

If our eyes, ears and feelings are our input source for information then the drivers, triggers and filters examined in this next section can go some way to helping us process and use it effectively.

Drivers, Triggers and Filters

I am not a psychology graduate so I will attempt to explain how I use these terms and how they might have an impact on our sessions. 'Jagreet and the Monkey' offers a framework for this explanation:

Jagreet and the Monkey

Jagreet arrives at the door of the session. He is with Tracy, a staff member, who is talking quietly to him and holding a stuffed monkey. Jags is nodding his head but his eyes never leave the monkey. As they enter the room, he is given the monkey, which he clutches tightly as he sits down. To me, the monkey is his driver. Its proximity and his feelings for it determine many of his responses. Throughout the session, Tracy negotiates with Jags to get the monkey into a safe enough position (sitting in his lap), which means that Jags feels safe, but also allows him to put both his hands on his drum and play.

If, for any reason, let's say Tracy was away and a different staff member attended the session and insisted on removing the monkey so Jags could play, this would cause an immediate stress response for Jagreet. Depending on his nature and personality, this could result in his breaking down in tears or becoming aggressive, both of which will affect his responses to the activities. The removal of the monkey is the trigger. Jags responds with a behaviour that has a consequence – if you do that, this will happen.

In my experience, staff are well-tuned to an individual's triggers. They work hard to make sure that they do not have a detrimental impact on their learning but, at the same time, try to manage them so that they are not reinforced unnecessarily in ways that would affect future learning or socialisation. This is a significant skill and, when done well, is a joy to watch.

Now, let's say that during the last session Jags attended, he had the monkey (driver) taken from him (trigger) and subsequently had an aggressive outburst (behaviour), which resulted in him having to be removed from the session (consequence). This week, he is unsure if this is going to be repeated – in his mind, he is replaying the incident from last session and he is anxious.

This anxiety becomes his filter, he sees everything leading up to the session through it and it will probably remain until he can replace it with a further positive experience to override the previous one. This filter may be session-specific, i.e. he becomes anxious just before the sessions. However, it is also possible that his anxiety level will permeate through other activities in his day, generally raising stress levels and making him unsettled.

Ideally, we want to replace the trigger, a major source of stress, with a driver that provides comfort and motivation, e.g. by incorporating a known favourite activity within the session, or by creating a role that provides motivation and esteem. "When it's time, I get to give the awards out." This means it's safe to leave monkey for a while as I have something important to do. This process is mapped out in the graphic below.

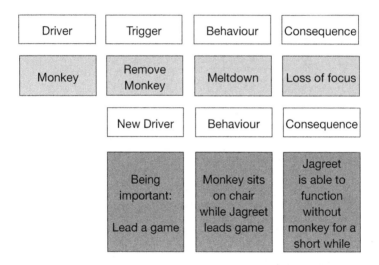

A note of caution here… be aware that the new driver may also come with its own triggers. Consequently, if you try to give someone else that role or job next week, it can result in dropping back to the trigger-behaviour-consequence routine. It is worth building in exit strategies in the shape of clear guidelines at the start, e.g. "You can give out the first three animals," or "You can do this week and X does next week." It's all about keeping the driver in mind and paying just enough homage to it to keep the player feeling safe whilst providing enough wriggle room to be creative.

Sometimes, the simplest solutions are the best and a phrase such as "First drumming and then monkey" can buy you enough time to get some drumming in. The player can let their monkey go (whatever form it may take) for a short time because they know it's coming back.

So, with our radar on, we should be able to gather information from our three primary sources – vision, hearing and feeling – giving us a picture of where we are now. Then, if we run this across our bank of drivers, triggers and filters, we have the information we need to plot going forward.

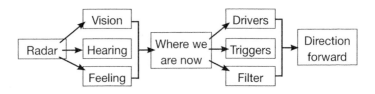

In the account below, there is an example of how this might look in action. Here, we are introduced to Kevin. Kevin likes drumming, but crossing the threshold of the activity room and sitting to start the activity causes him some difficulty, and it's almost possible to physically see the battle between his drivers and triggers as he tries to access the room.

Fishing for Kevin

My attempts to help Kevin into the room became rather like the process of casting a fishing line, hoping for a bite and then reeling in gingerly so as not to lose the catch before landing it on a drum. Kevin is part of a small group of drummers in a special school who meet for just half an hour a week to drum together. There are usually four or five pupils, two staff members and myself. Kevin is more than capable of engaging with all the activities and can, once in the room, make simple targeted choices and even shows a well-developed sense of humour. He rarely speaks and eye contact is fleeting, so I have to be careful to make but not sustain eye contact, as this causes him to backtrack either emotionally during the session, or physically if he's not actually made it into the room yet.

The process looks something like this…

First contact:

This is often made in the corridor on my way to the room. He anticipates my coming and makes a point of being somewhere our paths will cross. Brief eye contact and a verbal greeting from me and the game begins. He will walk up and down the corridor, looking in and smiling each time he passes the door; he loves to drum, but just cannot allow himself to cross the threshold spontaneously.

How long:

Sometimes, I manage to win him over as everyone else arrives but, more often than not, the fishing is done from my drum with him just outside the door. It usually involves asking a question or setting up a scenario that is thrown generally out into the air, "Who's going to give out the animals today?" Sometimes it has his name attached, sometimes not, but he knows it's for him and smiles. The game has begun and I have to accept that, at this stage, we are playing on his timescale, to his rules, but at least he's allowing me to play.

What is calling him into the room? (His driver – see page 47).

The need to play a specific drum:

"I wonder which drum Kevin will want to play? Think it's this one…" I usually try and avoid the one I know he likes and leave the option open for him. It usually works, but I have to go through the whole process until I get to his drum.

I want to be in charge of something, to have a role:

Sometimes I will use resources as bait. I'll leave a cuddly toy by the door – "I need the panda, I think it's by the door… can you bring it?" Sometimes it's quicker than others but one thing is for sure – if you move towards him or make it a challenge, the game is lost and the fish will not be landed this week.

Overall, this is quite a time-consuming exercise and can only work because it's a small group and the rest of the players are able to come in and start without prompting. However, staff report that drumming is one of his favourite activities of the week and his smile once he is in and drumming would seem to support this.

It is worth mentioning that all of us are governed by the driver-trigger-filter triangle, and a hard but necessary truth is that we need to do the work on ourselves as well. By doing this, it will be possible to ensure that we are governed by appropriate drivers and are responding rather than reacting to our triggers in order to achieve the best outcomes for everyone.

Do the work on yourself – a personal driver-trigger-filter scenario

Here are two possible alternatives:

1. Driver: I always want to deliver the best session I can. I have extremely high expectations for myself and take it to heart if I feel a session doesn't go well.
   Trigger: I misjudge a player's driver/trigger point and cause a player to react, having an impact on staff and the session.
   Filter: I begin to question my ability to read the next situation appropriately.
   Behaviour: Internally, I begin to question my radar.
   Consequence: I tense up and stop listening to my radar, instead focusing on my internal thoughts. This results in losing a large chunk of radar 'intelligence' material, hence I become less proactive and stay with

safe activities, which means we don't go to the edges where the sweet spots of learning are to be found.

Alternatively, the scenario could look like this:

2. Driver: I always want to deliver the best session I can and have extremely high expectations and take it to heart if a session doesn't go well.
    Trigger: I manage a trigger point well and facilitate a smooth transition through a player's anxiety.
    Filter: I can do this.
    Behaviour: I focus on input from my radar and am prepared to take a risk with a new activity.
    Consequences: Results in a new learning opportunity.

There is much more to be explored on this topic, but there is enough here to convince us that a good radar and a basic awareness of the driver-trigger-filter triangle are essential tools for quality connections with our players.

In conclusion, these are all foundational skills but they can be learned, and with practice can be absorbed to a subconscious level where they become just another layer of professional practice.

Summary: The Art of Connection

1. Use local knowledge.
2. Manage emotions.
3. Use your radar (eyes, ears, feelings/drivers, triggers, filters).
4. Remember to do the work on yourself.

CHAPTER 4

Programme Development

The programme development and principles outlined here are specifically designed for this client group, but have been drawn from a wealth of experience in all areas of the general community. Many of the activities will easily cross boundaries between different community groups, with simple modifications to delivery style or content.

The activities within the programme are loosely designed on a tiered four-level approach, giving an incremental series of activities that can be used to match different group levels. However, in practice, there will be a large amount of crossover and blurring of lines, not least because the likelihood of any group being made up of individuals at exactly the same developmental stage is very remote. Therefore, it may be necessary to pull in or modify activities from different levels in order to meet the group's needs. This needs-based approach is vital, so don't be afraid to play with the structure and modify things to make them work in your situation.

Task-Analysis Approach

One of the key foundations of this programme development returns to the original concept of intention-setting for the group or session. This begins with the simple question, "What do we want you to be able to do and how can we get you there?" This is where a task-analysis approach can be useful, as it prompts us to begin with the end goal and then break down the steps to master in order to achieve it.

Here are two definitions of the task analysis process, the second being possibly more suited to this context:

> "A process of determining the underlying abilities required and the structure of motor skills that need to be performed to complete a task." – Oxford English Dictionary of Sports Science and Medicine

> "Task analysis is the analysis of how a task is accomplished, including a detailed description of both manual and mental activities, task and element duration, task frequency, task allocation, task complexity and environmental conditions." – Wikipedia

Using this definition, we can then apply a light-touch task analysis to enable the identification of the primary target area for our programme. Here is a simplified example:

> Goal: To be able to play together and keep a steady beat.

> In order to be able to do this, players need to be able to:

- Comfortably access their drum.
- Hear and focus on a steady beat.

- Make physical contact with the drum repetitively in time with the beat.
- Sustain a regular pattern and intervals between the beat.
- Obtain sufficient contact with the drum to create appropriate sound.

By looking at these activities that combine to enable us to achieve the desired goal, we are able to identify key factors that may be missing. For example, if players are unable to hear and focus on a steady beat, action can be taken to establish and reinforce this key activity. This could be as simple as providing a larger, louder drum to provide the main or pulse beat.

By identifying tasks in this way, it is possible to focus quickly on which programme elements are needed to support development.

Programme Overlay Map

In order to keep this overlay as simple and as usable as possible, it has been restricted in this manual to two factors that have been identified as having a key influence on programme development and delivery. They are cognitive agility and engageability (latest addition to the Talking Rhythms technical dictionary!). The following sections define how these are used in this context.

Cognitive Agility:

In the context of our discussion, this refers to the ability and speed with which information can be held and processed. If care is not taken then the number of cognitive processes that are layered onto players can quickly mount up and cause overload for them. This can then result in confusion and frustration or simply messy music with no corporate structure.

Cognitive layers build quickly, each requiring additional processing ability:

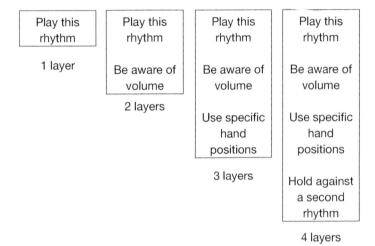

Play this rhythm	Play this rhythm	Play this rhythm	Play this rhythm
1 layer	Be aware of volume	Be aware of volume	Be aware of volume
	2 layers	Use specific hand positions	Use specific hand positions
		3 layers	Hold against a second rhythm
			4 layers

There are many factors affecting cognitive agility, from linguistic understanding, awareness of key concepts such as fast or slow, or processing of less concrete, more conceptual language.

For example, a phrase such as, "Play on 'the side' of your drum" may lead to players playing on the shell of the drum rather than the edge of the playing surface as intended. It is important that language is kept as uncluttered as possible and that potentially ambiguous words and phrases are clearly explained and rehearsed. A phrase such as "Make it rain on your drum," meaning to tap lightly with your fingertips, will result in quite a different response if the phrase is understood literally. Once the language is clear and words understood, reference must also be given to the amount of time it takes to process that information. This will have a direct impact on a player's response on the drum and their physical movement.

The word elephant, for example, may be clearly broken down into three syllables requiring a beat for each, el-e-phant, but a player's cognitive agility may mean that they only hear and play two syllables el(e)phant, the middle beat being lost in processing.

'Voice to Hand' – A Quick Diagnostic Tool:

This process of correctly transferring syllables from spoken word to drum is one that I refer to in shorthand as 'Voice to Hand', and it is very useful as a diagnostic tool. The accuracy of translating syllables from voice to hand is a good indicator of a number of factors, as it is linked to:

- Cognitive agility – the ability to separate different syllables and place them in an appropriate pattern.
- Motor skills – being able to control muscle responses to reproduce correct rhythms.
- Focus and attention – the overall ability to understand the task and maintain sufficient focus to complete accurately.

This diagnostic function of the voice-to-hand concept provides instant feedback on where to focus our activity levels. Take the three-stage process of rhythm generation: rhythm loop, rhythm phrase and rhythm sentence (Ch 1, p 4). In this context, a player with poor voice-to-hand responses will need the consolidation of rhythm loop activities with a variety of multiple syllable words. In contrast, accurate voice-to-hand responses mean that more complex rhythm sentences will be achievable.

It can be seen, then, that cognitive agility or processing speed will be a key factor in programme speed and development. Running in tandem with this is the notion of engageability, i.e. how much is the player willing or able to engage with the programme demands.

This is broken down into two areas:

- **Physical engageability**

In this case, it may be that the player has some form of physical restriction that impairs the ability to engage with an activity or programme. It may involve visual or auditory factors, or muscular or co-ordination issues. For example, significant restriction in the movement of one hand or arm that prevents use of two hands on the drum. It is important here to understand fully the nature of the restriction with advice from staff or medical professionals. There may be ways in which practice of movement through drumming may assist development of movement, but if this is not the case, the other option is to add programme modifications.

This can be done either with the activity or the delivery system, i.e. focus on rhythms that can be produced single-handedly or provide an appropriate beater for the drum. Here, the player is willing to engage, but the programme needs to accommodate restrictions in order to provide best access.

• Social engageability

In the context of social engageability, this situation may be reversed in that there are no physical restrictions to accessing activities, but other social or behavioural factors are at play that make it more difficult for the player to engage.

In this category, there are two further strands: an inability to engage because of personal social constraints or anxieties, or an unwillingness to engage manifested by obstructive or resistant behaviours. In making the distinction between these behavioural responses, it is an attempt to distinguish between:

1. The player who is caught in an internal cycle of compulsive thoughts or behaviours or who may have a predilection towards ritualistic behaviours that govern certain activities; and
2. The player who is acting out behaviours as a response to external factors in their life and may have developed patterns of aggression or resistance.

At its simplest, this is the difference between "I can't play this drum because, when I touch it, the surface is rough," which is a tactile sensory response, or "I'm not playing this drum, it's stupid, the whole thing's stupid," which is an emotional response. As an emotional response, this may have a myriad of drivers from fear of failure, lack of sleep, or resistance to authority, "You can't make me do something I don't want to do."

Clearly, each of these responses will need to be approached differently and will have a direct impact upon programme development. The biggest challenge, as previously mentioned, is that these rarely happen in isolation and any group may contain one or more of each category. So, whilst the following offers a map over which to plot a programme, the lines between programmes and activities will by necessity be blurred in reality.

Programme Overlay Map

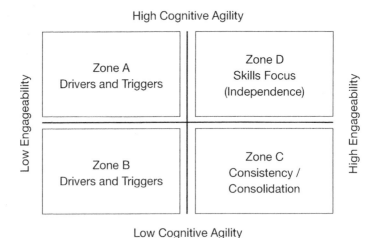

Groups within all of these zones will have many common needs, not least the need for structure, clarity of instructions, activity cues, and flexible delivery styles. However, groups within each zone will bring with them particular needs that will be a priority for their programme.

In the charts below are some suggestions for the priority areas for programme development in each zone. The lists and descriptors are not designed to be exhaustive, but to give an overview of the sorts of background elements that will drive the programme in that zone.

The first two Zones, A and B, are taken together, as the baseline elements are very similar and have the most impact from the low engageability factor of these zones.

Zone	Main Programme Characteristics	Key Programme Influences
A. High Cognitive Agility Low Engageability	Attention to Drivers and Triggers	Physical: - Environment - Touch & sound sensitivities - Individual physical adaptions - Personal compulsions or rituals
B. Low Cognitive Agility Low Engageability		Social/Behavioural: - Clear ground rules/ boundaries - Calm consistent approach - Explicit expectations - Support self esteem - Appropriate levels of technical challenge

Although the main programme characteristics are the same for both of these zones, the main difference between them will become evident when stability is achieved within programme delivery. In Zone A, once drivers and triggers have been identified and addressed as best as possible, then technical ability and programme content will move quickly through the levels. In Zone B, players will need longer to consolidate activities and develop new areas. Increments will need to be smaller and well-rehearsed. In a note of caution, these groups can take time to settle and, even when settled, can slip quickly between levels of engageability depending on mood and external circumstances.

The final two zones stand alone and will be very different in content and pace of delivery.

Zone	Main Programme Characteristics	Key Programme Influences
C.High Engageability Low Cognitive Agility	Consistency and Consolidation	- Clear visuals and cues - Repetition and consolidation - Small steps, known to unknown - Consistency of delivery style and content

Here, the challenges to programme delivery come mostly from retention of previous skills and knowledge, which need to be rehearsed in order to consolidate them. It's useful to group activities under focused concepts. For example, it is possible to practise fast or slow with a variety of different activity inputs (e.g. say your name quickly, walk around the circle slowly, play your drum really fast). This prevents the session becoming dry and repetitive whilst still consolidating previous knowledge.

Zone	Main Programme Characteristics	Key Programme Influences
D. High Cognitive Agility High Engageability	Skills Focus Developing Independence	- Increased technical challenge - Layering of rhythms and cognitive elements - Creating personal rhythms - Increased interpersonal interactions - Developing sense of musicality

Zone D provides the least individual player constraints and offers the opportunity to increase interpersonal contact and develop players' own independent skills. This zone allows the opportunity to layer different rhythms and activities as players become able to hold one rhythm against another, thus blending patterns together. The cognitive agility levels within this group also means that players are able to hold multiple layers of cognitive challenge at the same time, i.e. playing a technically accurate piece against a counter-rhythm.

These three key elements provide an efficient toolbox with which to build our programme foundations:

- Individual drivers and triggers.
- Cognitive agility and engageability.
- Task-analysis approach.

Session Map

Having established our programme foundations, let us turn to the construction of our session. The sessions are constructed using five programme elements or headings under which to place our activities. These elements are:

- Intro / starters – opening connections.
- Tech / dynamics – hand skills / musicality.
- Rhythm generation – creating rhythms / visual or auditory cues.
- Games – consolidation activities.
- Songs – vocal or rhythm songs or patterns.

At the end of this manual (appendix p.75) there is a selection of activity cards relating to activities identified under these elements. Below is a card from Intro / Starters Level 1. The level, programme elements and activity instructions are all contained on the card.

Lion, Octopus, Panda, Duck: Activity Cards

Who's got the Monkey?

Level: 1	Programme element: **Intro / starters**	Resources: **Cuddly monkey (or creature of choice)**	Strand
Description	**Monkey is given to or placed at the feet of a player**		

Everyone plays:

Who's got the monkey, who's got the monkey,

Who's got the monkey, (Name) has.

The player with the monkey then demonstrates their drum with whatever beats or style they wish to or can manage.

The focus here is that we get to hear each player's 'voice' (drum) and that we get to practise listening to others.

The activity cards are graded in four levels and offer a variety of activities that can be slotted together to create an initial programme for groups from each of the four programme overlay map zones. Here is an example of a level one session programme. The programme element headings help to provide clarity when planning and choosing activities and give a clear focus to each section of the session.

Group name: _____ Time Approx. 40 Min			
Intro / starter	Rhythm generation	Tech / dynamics	Game
Hello Monkey	Animal Rhythm 1	Fast & Slow	Pass the Rumble

There is a further piece of information on the activity cards in the form of an icon on the right-hand side of the card under 'strand'. This refers to a series of developmental strands that underpin the focus of a particular activity and tie them back into our original intention setting and task analysis.

The strands and icons are listed below, along with a brief description of each strand's purpose:

Lion, Octopus, Panda, Duck: *Developmental Strands*

	Pulse generation	Activities designed to develop and consolidate playing in time with a common pulse or beat. Will be revisited at all levels of playing, but essential at level 1.
	Voice-to-hand	"If you can say it, you can play it." Voice-to-hand is a useful diagnostic tool indicating players' cognitive agility and processing skills. It also links closely with development of syllables and phonological attention. V = Great big elephant; H = / / ///
	Attention & focus	Activities or strategies designed to capture attention, refocus attention or train listening accuracy. Including playing-together skills, being ready for your turn, playing one rhythm against another.
	Peer-to-peer	Designed to encourage direct communication between peers either 1/1 choosing who plays next, passing the rumble. Sharing verbally our ideas and feelings or conducting whole group dynamics.
	Cognitive agility	These activities will be focused on either identifying technical levels of capability or as ways of building players' ability to apply skills learned from activities.
	Motor skills	Integrated activities designed to rehearse and enhance both gross and fine motor skills. These are graduated up through the levels from basic timekeeping, using alternate hands, identifying left and right and making accurate technical placements for different tone sounds.

This adds the final layer to our programme. For example, in our initial analysis we identified that accurately matching syllables to drum beats still needs work. Therefore, the focus will need to be on activities that rehearse and support 'voice-to-hand' consolidation. Likewise, if we want to enhance peer-to-peer communication then the main section of our session is going to be focused on activities to support this.

In this next example of a Level 2 card on animal rhythms, it can be seen that the activity has input on four of the development strands. The activity is technical, so involves a degree of required attention and focus.

There is a clear voice-to-hand element in the focus on syllable reproduction. The requirement of specific hand positions requires both cognitive agility and motor skills.

It is clear then that one simple, well-designed activity appropriately matched to the group can provide an impressive depth of kinaesthetic learning.

Lion, Octopus, Panda, Duck: Activity Cards

	Animal Rhythms 2		Strand
Level: **2**	Programme element:	Resources:	
	Tech / dynamics	**Visual animal cue**	
Description	**Key Principle: Allocating hand positions to syllable beats**		

Using animal of choice, create a simple rhythm sentence for them appropriate to the players' cognitive levels and motor skills, e.g. 'Great big elephant'

Allocate hand positions: Middle = **M** (Bass) Side = **S** (Tone)

M   M   S   S   S

'**Great big elephant**'

NB – this is a good point to introduce use of alternate hands for each beat, as this provides a good platform for future playing.

Create hand patterns for your favourite animal rhythms.

69

At this point, you could be forgiven for thinking that my session planning is accompanied by hours of diligent paperwork and preparation, and that I have books of pre-prepared programmes set out in meticulous detail as prescribed here. Nothing could be further from the truth! What I've described here in *Lion, Octopus, Panda, Duck* are the paradigms and protocols that underpin the way in which I work. In order to lay them out, it was necessary to commit them to word form in this way. In practice, it's a much more dynamic, in-the-moment process.

Dynamic In-the-Moment Programme Development

One of the key points of my personal development and provider of the most profound learning curves is the moment when someone says "We've had a swap around, the Minibeasts are coming instead." The Minibeasts are a group of 6-7-year-olds, hitherto unknown to you and new to drumming. It's at this point when they arrive in front of you and you realise that none of the things you have done this term will work. Your resources are either too small, too big, too complicated, not engaging enough or overstimulating. Time to do a little task analysis and ask yourself, "What can we do?"

When presented with such a situation recently, in the first session it quickly became apparent that the group's attention span was such that 'everyone with a drum' was not going to produce anything meaningful. The key starting intention was going to be to try and get everyone to do something together, at the same time – still a tall order.

So, the second session saw just two drums, mine and a turn-taker's drum. We took it in turns to try drumming a simple pulse rhythm together while everyone clapped along. Singing our favourite song helped, and at least we had our starting point. Clapping moved to jumping in time and stomping on circles placed on the floor. Red and green circles were introduced for stop and go and, gradually, week by week, the programme developed.

These can be the most stressful and petrifying times of your facilitation career, but they will surely be the points at which you grow the most, and your repertoire and library of activities will be given depth and versatility.

Summary

The intention for these development tools is for them to be used as a scaffold on which to grow an organic, flexible and responsive programme. I created a series of activities that support players' needs and provide structure and developmental progression by the use of:

- Task-analysis approaches.
- Mapping players' needs and activities on programme overlay zones.
- Identifying priority development strands.
- Assembling appropriate programme elements.

Conclusion

It seems a long way from the travelling band of soft toys with which we began our journey but, in essence, what this manual has done is to prepare the stage ready for their appearance. On the face of it, the end result looks like simply using cuddly toys to create rhythms; however, the success of the end product, personal growth, and development of language and social communication is built on these foundations.

Throughout the manual, the steps have been put into place to build the protocols that will guide effective programme delivery by:

Preparation:

- Taking account of environment and setup.
- Setting intentions.

Understanding needs:

- The nature and individual needs of the client group.
- Being aware of drivers and triggers.

Interpretation of input:

- Making use of our radar.
- Using local intelligence.

Managing functions:

- Learning to respond rather than react.
- Viewing players in a holistic context.

Matching programme elements:

- The use of programme overlays and development strands.

These five principles, once understood, can be applied quickly and flexibly in any situation, allowing for well-grounded but spontaneous responses to dynamic situations.

A final word

I am fully aware that we have only touched on many of the areas that have been identified in this manual owing to a need to keep things manageable and succinct. However, I hope that I have fulfilled my intention to provide a solid, workable framework on which to develop and deliver an effective programme.

Please heed the call to take and use what works for you, leave out what doesn't, and extend and modify anything to suit your needs.

APPENDIX

Activity Cards

Introduction

Each of the activity cards included here is designed to offer an activity idea in one of the five different programme elements (p.65). They can be used systematically to create a short progressive activity programme, or used as stand alone activities as needed.

Whilst each card is a complete activity, there is always room for modification or development depending on your group, style or available resources. By extending the activities in this way you will quickly develop a programme that is tailored to your needs and your situation.

Finally, remember:

> Keep sight of your intentions
> and have fun whenever possible!

Lion, Octopus, Panda, Duck: Programme Overview

	Title: Name of activity	Resources:	Strand
Level:	Programme element:	**Additional**	**Indicates**
1 – 4	**Intro / starters**: opening connections	**resources**	**focused**
to indicate	**Tech / dynamics**: hand skills/musicality		**outcomes**
degree of	**Rhythm generation**: cues and resources		
necessary	**Games**: consolidation activities		See Key
skills	**Songs**: vocal / rhythm songs and patterns		below
Description	**Key focus of activity**		
	Description of activities and facilitator's notes/cues		

Pulse generation	Attention & focus	Cognitive agility

Voice-to-hand	Peer-to-peer	Motor skills

Lion, Octopus, Panda, Duck: *Developmental Strands*

♥	Pulse generation	Activities designed to develop and consolidate playing in time with a common pulse or beat. Will be revisited at all levels of playing, but essential at level 1.
🐆	Voice-to-hand	"If you can say it, you can play it." Voice-to-hand is a useful diagnostic tool indicating players' cognitive agility and processing skills. It also links closely with development of syllables and phonological attention. V = Great big elephant; H = / / ///
📢	Attention & focus	Activities or strategies designed to capture attention, refocus attention or train listening accuracy. Including playing-together skills, being ready for your turn, playing one rhythm against another.
👥	Peer-to-peer	Designed to encourage direct communication between peers either 1/1 choosing who plays next, passing the rumble. Sharing verbally our ideas and feelings or conducting whole group dynamics.
🐙	Cognitive agility	These activities will be focused on either identifying technical levels of capability or as ways of building players' ability to apply skills learned from activities.
🦆	Motor skills	Integrated activities designed to rehearse and enhance both gross and fine motor skills. These are graduated up through the levels from basic timekeeping, using alternate hands, identifying left and right and making accurate technical placements for different tone sounds.

Level 1

Animal Rhythms

Level: 1	Programme element:	Resources:	Strand
	Rhythm generation	**Visual cue for animal of choice**	
Description	**Key Principle: "Anything you can say, you can play!"** Using an animal of choice, create a simple rhythm sentence for them, appropriate to the players' cognitive levels and motor skills, e.g. **'Hippo' or 'Great big elephant'.** Make sure that the syllables each have a beat allocated to them and encourage players to play them accurately: **Hi ppo Great big el e phant** **1 2 1 2 3 & 4** (If players are comfortable, ask individuals to demonstrate for the group.)	

			Strand
Fast / Slow Loud / Quiet			
Level: **1**	Programme element: **Tech / dynamics**	Resources: **Auditory or visual cues as appropriate**	
Description	**Understanding changes in volume or tempo and responding appropriately to cued changes**		
	Using a simple animal rhythm (see Animal Rhythms L1), demonstrate and practise the signals for two contrasting levels of your chosen set 'Fast / Slow' or 'Loud / Quiet'. Once demonstrated, allow a player to come to the centre and control the beat by making changes between the two levels.		
	This activity lends itself well to making choices, either by offering to a player in verbal or cue card form, 'Do you want to play Slow or Fast?', play slow or fast, allowing them to make changes for the group.		

	Hello Monkey		
Level: **1**	Programme element: **Intro / starters**	Resources: **Cuddly toy monkey** (or creature of choice)	Strand
Description	**Leader holds monkey and asks who wants to see monkey first. As monkey is handed over, everyone says....** "Hello _____ my name's monkey," and then play: **Mon key mon key oo oo ah ah** Drum drum drum drum (make monkey gesture) "Choose a friend..." Player then chooses where monkey goes next.		

How Many Beats?		Strand
Level: 1	Programme element: **Games**	Resources: **Large foam dice or number cards 1 - 6**	
Description	**Accurately representing beats for different number cues** Player rolls dice or selects number card and reads out the number. Either player or leader then shouts out the number and everyone plays the correct number of beats. 5! 1 2 3 4 5 6! 1 2 3 4 5 6 bananas! To ensure accurate stop at the end, a shout could be added to mark end of count. This could either be a simple 'stop!' or a random word of choice for fun.	

Jump Spots		Strand
Level: 1	Programme element: **Games**	Resources: **Coloured spots or markers for the floor**	
Description	**Embody pulse beats by taking it to movement first**		
	Create a simple regular pulse beat at an appropriate tempo for players.		
	With markers placed appropriately on the floor, model jumping from marker to marker, landing on each marker in time with the beat.		
	If two-feet jumping is a challenge, players could step from spot to spot.		
	The key is to work towards accurate timing with pulse.		
	Add 'follow the leader', 'jump freeze', 'speed up slow down', 'change direction' to suit		

Pass the Rumble		Strand
Level: 1		
Programme element:	Resources:	
Games	No additional resources	
Description	**Fun, basic attention-grabber, awareness of others, making choices**	

Teach 'rumble'. Can be done in middle or at edge of drum or used with shaker or percussion. Can even be done on tabletop or on knees. Players play as fast as possible on cue. (Encourage speed not volume and be aware of hand care.)

Don't forget to teach **STOP** signal!

Leader takes rumble and says **"I've got the rumble."** Make sure that everyone knows only you can play. Then, you can pass the rumble to another player who then rumbles before passing it on.

It often helps to reduce choices for players when faced with a whole group.

"Do you want (name) or (name)?"

Level: 1	Programme element:	Play 4 Stop 4		
		Resources:		Strand
	Tech / dynamics	**Visual stop 'cue' if necessary**		
Description	**Develop early beat recognition and practice cognitive and motor skills to control stop and start pattern**			
	Establish constant pulse beat: 1 2 3 4 / 1 2 3 4 / 1 2 3 4.			
	Introduce stop with appropriate visual/auditory cue: 1 2 3 4 stop / 1 2 3 4 stop.			
	Add count to end of stop to reintroduce beat.			
	1 2 3 4 STOP 23 GO 1 2 3 4 STOP 23 GO 1 2 3 4 STOP etc.			

Pulse Walking		
Level: 1	Programme element: **Intro / starters**	Resources: **Space to move**	Strand
Description	**A simple, fun activity with two beneficial outcomes** **– Create energy and personal interaction** **– Offer visual diagnostic of pulse awareness** Once a good strong group pulse (marching beat) has been established within the group, individuals take it in turns to enter centre of the circle and step in time with the group pulse. Difficulty maintaining a regular step pattern may suggest issues either with cognitive processing, or physical co-ordination. Lots of opportunity for reinforcement of pulse is essential. Variations might include: – player choosing next walker – varying speed of pulse – adding 'stops', e.g. 3 beats stop (rpt)	

Rhythm Gym

Level: 1	Programme element:	Resources:	Strand
	Intro / starters	No additional	
Description	**A good adaptable activity combining two modalities:**		
	– drumming		
	– and movement		
	This follows on well from Play 4 Stop 4 as it uses the same basic framework.		
	Introduce Play 4 Stop 4.		
	This time, in place of silent 4, add 4 movements for second group of beats.		
	Add 4 movements for the second group of beats.		
	1 2 3 4 Reach reach reach rpt.		
	Variation: clap instead of movement.		
	Add combinations of movements.		
	1 2 3 4 Clap, knee, head, drum.		

87

Stomp Walk Run		
Programme element: **Games**	Resources: **Space to move**	Strand
Description	**Embody pulse beats and tempo changes in time with drum beats**	

Demonstrate three visual representations of the tempos STOMP WALK RUN.

Connect these to drum rhythms for given cue:

Stomp stomp stomp stomp   Step step step step step step   Run!

1   2   3   4   1 & 2 & 3 & 4 (as fast as is safe)

The cues for this activity can be switched:

– Drummers take cue from feet of the walker and match tempo accordingly.

– Walker responds to the beat of the drums and matches movements.

Level: 1	Programme element: **Tech / dynamics**	**Stop / Go**		Strand
		Resources: **Red and green symbol cards or floor spots**		
Description	**Encourage visual awareness and connection with group activities**			
	Player comes to centre and either stands by or holds symbol for Go.			
	Everyone plays (either simple pulse beat or rumble – as fast as you can).			
	Player in centre changes symbol or moves to red spot Stop all stop!			
	This activity lends itself to range of support levels.			
	Start level: adult moving with player between stop and go and registering that it is their actions that are causing the change in sound.			
	Higher level: conductor is aware of concept and 'plays' with commands to elicit response from players.			

Wake Up Drum		
Level: 1	Programme element: **Intro / starters**	Resources: **Drums for players**	Strand
Description	**Can be used as a default entry point for each session, gives players a cue that the session has started, and used at end gives exit point framing the session.** Once players are seated at drum begin with: **Stroke your drum with 1 hand** (Players run their hand around the head of the drum) **Now the other hand** **Now both hands** **Make it rain** (Players 'tickle' the centre of the drum) **Rain on the side** / at edge of playing surface **Rain in the middle** / in centre of drum Lead into single-handed pulse beat in centre of drum / follow with alternate hands.	

Who's got the Monkey?		
Level: 1	Programme element: **Intro / starters**	Resources: **Cuddly monkey (or creature of choice)**	Strand
Description	**Monkey is given to or placed at the feet of a player**		
	Everyone plays: Who's got the monkey, who's got the monkey, Who's got the monkey, (Name) has.		
	The player with the monkey then demonstrates their drum with whatever beats or style they wish to or can manage.		
	The focus here is that we get to hear each player's 'voice' (drum) and that we get to practise listening to others.		

Lion, Octopus, Panda, Duck: *Song cards*

Humpty Dumpty

Programme element:	Resources:	Additional Activities/Actions
Songs	**No additional**	
Humpty Dumpty sat on a wall	'cause Humpty Dumpty bungee jumped	This is a call-and-response song, so each line is sung by a leader and called back by group.
Humpty Dumpty had a great fall	Say "boing" x2	
All the king's horses and all the king's men	Say "get me down" x 2	This means that there is very little learning involved and it is quick and easy to get up to speed.
Couldn't put humpty together again	Say "aaaaaaaaaaaaaaah!"	
Say "ah!" x2	Humpty Dumpty sat on a wall	I often lead this with a simple djembe drum rhythm. This allows us to add a dance section in between verses.
Say "ah ah ah" x2	Humpty Dumpty had a great fall	
Say "aaaaaaaaaaaaaaaaaaaaah!"	He didn't whine and he didn't cry	If space is at a premium, we do 'Bottom dancing', i.e. bottom and feet stay where they are but top half can dance how it likes!
	'cause Humpty Dumpty's learned to fly	Ask someone to come up and lead the 'Say' responses in voices and styles of their own for group to copy.
Humpty Dumpty sat on a wall	Say "All aboard" x2	Once learned: Ask group to repeat the response in exactly same manner as call. Then vary the call using:
Humpty Dumpty had a great fall	Say "Chocks away" x2	– **different voices**
He didn't get bruised and he didn't get bumped	Say" eeeeeeaaawwww!"	– **different pitches**
		– **different volumes**

Level 2

Level: **2**	4 Middle – 4 Side		
	Programme element:	Resources:	Strand
	Intro / starters	**No additional**	
Description	Introduction to key hand positions on the drum		
	Identify the **middle** of the drum and play:		
	STOMP STOMP STOMP .... (elephant).........flat hand in centre of the drum.		
	Identify the **edge** or side of drum and play:		
	Tap tap tap tap ....(tiny mouse).....place fingers on edge of drum (2nd knuckle to tip).		
	NB – be aware of finger safety – fingers together, hitting drum flat, no excessive impact.		
	Play together:		
	4 in the middle 4 on the side		
	1 2 3 4 / 1 2 3 4		

93

Animal Choices / Numbers

Level: **2**	Programme element:	Resources:	Strand
		Cuddly animals or familiar objects, dice and number cards to 6	
Description	**Key Principle:** Managing turn-taking and choice-making		
	Game		
	Choose six cuddly animals and line them up across the floor numbering from one to six using number cards.		
	1 2 3 4 5 6		
	Hippo Frog Tiger Elephant Crow Penguin		
	Each player takes a turn to roll the dice and identify the number and then the associated animal. **The whole group plays animal rhythm song together.** (Rpt)		
	NB – use a variety of syllables in animal names to differentiate for players.		

Animal Compass

		Strand
Level: 2	Programme element: **Rhythm generation**	Resources: **Cuddly animals or familiar objects**
Description	**Conducting group activity through movement / visual cues**	
	Choose four animals and revisit their rhythm songs with the group.	
	Place the animals in compass positions in the centre of the floor.	
	Conductor stands in the middle of the circle.	
	When the conductor moves towards an animal, the group responds with the appropriate rhythm song.	Owl
		Penguin Tiger
		Octopus
	NB – to start with, bring the conductor back to the centre each time and encourage the group to stop between rhythms.	

Animal Rhythms 2

Level: **2**	Programme element: **Tech / dynamics**	Resources: **Visual animal cue**	Strand
Description	**Key Principle:** **Allocating hand positions to syllable beats** Using animal of choice, create a simple rhythm sentence for them appropriate to the players' cognitive levels and motor skills, e.g. **'Great big elephant'** Allocate hand positions: Middle = **M** (Bass) Side = **S** (Tone) M M S S S **'Great big elephant'** **NB – this is a good point to introduce use of alternate hands for each beat, as this provides a good platform for future playing.** Create hand patterns for your favourite animal rhythms.		

Drum / Shake

Level: 2	Programme element: **Tech / dynamics**	Resources: **Handheld shakers (egg shakers are good)**	Strand
Description	**Great activity for promoting gross motor skills** **– Focus on independence of hands in activities** Holding shaker in one hand and other hand on centre of drum. Play and say: **drum** **shake** swap shaker and repeat – Start slow and **increase tempo**. – Play three and change: **Drum / shake** **drum / shake** **drum / shake** **change hands**		

	Favourite Foods		Strand
Level: 2	Programme element: **Rhythm generation**	Resources: **No additional**	
Description	**Key Principle:** **Anything you can say, you can play!** Revise rhythm song **Fish and chips** Ask players for examples of their favourite foods and create rhythm songs and play each one with the group. **'Beans on toast'** **'Rice Crispies'** **'Sausages'** **'Pizza pizza pepperoni pizza'** (Size and cognitive level of group will determine how many songs you can create in a session. At this stage, more than four songs are probably enough to cause overload). If the group is able to construct songs and hold the patterns, you might want to move on to **favourite foods / layering**.		

	Favourite food / side to side		Strand
Level: 2	Programme element: **Rhythm generation**	Resources: **No additional**	
Description	**Key Principle:** **Playing appropriately on cue, responding to others**		
	Choose two favourite food rhythm phrases.		
	Divide the group into two halves and allocate a rhythm song to each half.		
	Practice their songs with each half playing one pattern and stopping at the end each time. Once songs are established, group one plays their song once immediately followed by group two, **swapping songs between sides**		
	For more fun:		
	– Place a conductor in the centre and allow a group to play until the conductor turns and signals next group to start.		
	– Add more groups!		

99

Fish and Chips

Level: **2**	Programme element: **Tech / dynamics**	Resources: **No additional**	Strand

Description	**Practising key hand positions on the drum**
	
	Recap on 4 Middle – 4 Side (see activity card)
	
	Introduce rhythm song **Fish and chips**
	
	   1 2 3 (rest)
	
	Play first beat (fish) in the middle of the drum and 2nd two (and chips) on side
	
	   Fish and chips
	
	   M S S (rest)
	
	NB – make sure that **alternate hands** are used for each beat.
	
	(Note: middle / side equates to bass / tone sounds of drum.)		

Me First Play 4 Stop 4		Strand
Level: **2**	Programme element:	Resources:
	Intro / starters	**No additional**
Description	**Extension to Play 4, Stop 4, introducing call and response**	
	Recap Play 4 Stop 4	
	1 2 3 4 STOP 2 3 GO 1 2 3 4 STOP 2 3 GO 1 2 3 4 STOP etc.	
	Introduce concept of **me first – then you**	
	(Use additional language signs or symbols as appropriate)	
	Let's play **me 2 3 4 you 2 3 4**	

101

Play Your Drum

	Programme element:	Resources:	Strand
Level: 2	**Intro / starters**	**No additional**	
Description	**Group activity focusing on hearing an individual player's 'voice'**		
	Song / chant (and play)		
	Play your drum	**Play your drum**	
	Play your drum	**Play your drum**	
	Play your drum	**Play your drum**	
	Stop	**Hannah**	
	Once the chant's established, add a player's name and encourage them in a short solo so we can hear their voice.		

			Strand
	Tempo Traffic Lights		
Level: **2**	Programme element:	Resources:	
	Tech / dynamics	**Coloured markers: red, yellow and green**	
Description	**Activity for individual leader to conduct changes**		
	– Making accurate changes in speed		
	– Connecting with group changes on cue		
	Stop / Go		
	– Introduce red and green markers and practice stop / go.		
	– Hold markers up for group to follow stop / go changes.		
	– Place markers on floor and nominate player to step between the two.		
	Fast / slow / stop		
	– Introduce yellow marker – focus on attention to changes so that group changes are as together as possible.		

103

Lion, Octopus, Panda, Duck: *Song cards*

Programme element:	Simple Song	
Songs	Resources: **No additional**	Additional Activities/Actions
Sing me a simple song		Can be sung unaccompanied or with a simple drum beat:
Sing me a simple song	Play on drum or clap.	
Not too short	Sing me a silly song	B B B B
Not too long	Sing me a silly song	Sing me a simple song
Sing me a simple song	Not too short	
	Not too long	This is a call-and-response section.
Oh yeah (Oh yeah)	Sing me a silly song	
Oh yeah (Oh yeah)	Blah blah (Blah blah)	Once players have the hang of it, different voices can be used for each call and copied by players.
Oh yeah (Oh yeah)	Nah nah (Nah nah)	
Sing me a simple song (Cha	Boo hoo (Boo hoo)	
cha cha)	Sing me a silly song (Cha cha cha)	Build confidence by allowing players to take it in turns to lead call and response with their own voices.

Lion, Octopus, Panda, Duck: *Song cards*

Programme element:	Resources:	Additional Activities/Actions
Songs	**No additional**	
Sing me a noisy song	Play on drum or clap.	Can be sung unaccompanied or with a simple drum beat:
Sing me a noisy song	Sing me a quiet song	
Sing it loud	Sing me a quiet song	B B B B
Sing it strong	Don't wake the baby, his nappy pongs!	
Sing me a noisy song	Sing me a quiet song	Sing me a noisy song
Oh yeah (Oh yeah)	Blah blah (Blah blah)	This is a call-and-response section.
Oh yeah (Oh yeah)	Nah nah (Nah nah)	
Oh yeah (Oh yeah)	Boo hoo (Boo hoo)	Once players have the hang of it, different voices can be used for each call and copied by players.
Sing me a simple song (Cha cha cha)	Sing me a silly song (Cha cha cha)	
		Build confidence by allowing players to take it in turns to lead call and response with their own voices.

Simple Song: Additional Verses

Level 3

Animal Sentences 3		Strand
Level: **3**	Resources:	
Programme element:	Drums / visual cue animal cards	
Rhythm generation		
Combining syllables to create rhythm patterns		
Select a selection of cue cards with a variety of syllable lengths.		
Arrange in chosen order:		
Syllables **Hippo** **Octopus** **Zebra** **Owl**		
2 3 2 1		
Rearrange the syllable order to change rhythm pattern.		
Challenge players to find their own words to create their own patterns.		
Use with topic words to consolidate vocabulary acquisition.		

	Boom Boom / My Name		Strand
Level: **3**	Programme element:	Resources:	
	Intro / starters	**Clap or drum (or body percussion)**	
Description	**Increasing attention and awareness**		
	Begin by vocally rehearsing the phrase:		
	Boom boom my name, boom boom someone else		
	Once secure verbally, demonstrate use of drum and name:		
	Boom boom Simon boom boom Arti		
	Drum my name drum someone else		
	The player nominated (Arti) then repeats the process and passes the beat on.		

Double up Rumble

Level: **3**	Programme element: **Games**	Resources: **Drum**	Strand
Description	**Fun / attention and focus** Reintroduce pass the rumble as per level 1. In this game, when the rumble is passed to a player, the players to the right and left of the receiving player must also double up and rumble as well until the rumble is passed on.		

Double up

Rumble

Drum and Shake

		Strand
Programme element:	Resources:	
Tech / dynamics	**Drum and hand-held shaker**	

Level: 3

Description

Rehearse simple rhythm phrase with **shaker** in hand of choice, e.g.

Promoting independence in cognitive layers

```
    I   like  pi   zza
    1   2    3    4
```

Once established, add **drum** on 1 and 3 with other hand:

Shaker hand
```
    I   like  pi   zza
    1   2    3    4
```

Drum hand
```
    /        /
    1   2    3    4
```

Change hands and repeat.

– Start with drum first.
– Add harder shaker rhythm.

	Favourite Foods / Layering	Strand
Level: 3	Programme element: **Rhythm generation**	Resources: **No additional**
Description	**Using pulse to layer rhythm songs**	

Create a simple **pulse beat** with the group: **1 2 3 4**

Select a favourite food rhythm song and chant over the pulse beat:

Beans   on   toast

1   2   3   4

Demonstrate how different songs will fit over the same pulse:

I   eat   shredded   wheat

1   2   3 &   4

Now you have the glue! As long as each player plays their rhythm song in time with the pulse, you can build as many layers as you like. **NB – start with two!**

110

Fish and Chips and a Drink		Strand
Level: **3**	Programme element: **Rhythm generation**	Resources: **Drums**	
Description	**Generating extended rhythm sentences** Introduce fish and chip rhythm as per previous cards. Ask players to suggest a drink they would like with their fish and chips. This allows for exploration and extension of rhythms within players' capabilities. **Fish and chips and a lemonade** **Fish and chips and juice** **Fish and chips and a little bit of milkshake** (For additional focus, add specific hand patterns to created rhythms).	

111

Fish, No Chips!			
Level: 3	Programme element:	Resources:	Strand
Description	**Tech / dynamics**	**Drums**	

Using key hand positions on the drum / reacting to rhythm changes

Rehearse 'Fish and Chips' as per level 2.

Fish and chips

M S S (rest)

NB – make sure that **alternate hands** are used for each beat.

Once established and **while still playing**, announce that we have run out of fish.

'No fish!' Players now play the rhythm but place a rest where fish was.

(rest) and chips

Once fish is back in stock, repeat with 'chips' or even 'and' to challenge players.

Level: 3	Programme element: **Tech / dynamics**	Resources: **Drum, visual cue x4**	Strand

Middle or Side?

Description	**Developing use of bass and tone sounds (introducing composition)**	

Place visual cues in a line and rehearse the rhythm sentence,

e.g. **Monkey – Cow – Hippo – Zebra.**

Arrange the cues on two levels and designate one level bass / middle and one tone / side.

Middle ——— ——— ——— Bass

Side ——— ——— ——— Tone

Play with arrangements to change the rhythm patterns.

Missing Numbers

Level: 3	Programme element:	Resources:	Strand
	Games	**Drums / number cards 1 - 8**	
Description	**Awareness of number order/increase focus and attention**		
	Place number cards in order on the floor, play and count in time together.		
	1 2 3 4 5 6 7 8		
	Ask a player to **remove a number from the sequence and play again** missing out player's number.		
	1 2 ● 4 5 6 7 8		
	Change the position of missing number.		
	Removing two numbers allows for great variety of rhythm phrases.		

Red Spot		Strand
Level: 3		
Programme element:	Resources:	
Games	**Drums / red floor spot / cuddly toy x 4**	
Description		
Making choices while maintaining focus and attention		
Place the four animals in a line on the floor. Play animal sentence together. Once established, introduce red circle under animal of players' choice.		
Cow Penguin Hippo Duck		
Replay the rhythm sentence holding space for the red spot but without playing the word. Allow players to choose new position of red spot.		

Lion, Octopus, Panda, Duck: *Song cards*

Here's a Song We Like to Sing

Programme element: **Songs**	Resources: **Drums / voices**	Additional Activities/ Actions
A fun call-and-response song to introduce a performance with a small challenge for a drum beat	Drum beat **Here's a song we like to sing** / / / / **Puts rhythm in your feet lets you do your thing**	This a great starter or introduction piece.
Spoken rhythm sentences, in the style of US army drill call (repeat each line).	**Gonna stamp my feet and clap my hands** / / / **Gonna play my music all over this land** / / / /	Once repeated twice, when the song comes to an end, players can either break out into a rumble...
Here's a song we like to sing (Rpt) **Puts rhythm in your feet lets you do your thing** **Gonna stamp my feet and clap my hands** **Gonna play my music all over this land**		...or a simple count in 1 2 3 4 can lead into a prearranged groove or rhythm pattern.

116

Lion, Octopus, Panda, Duck: *Song cards*

Banana Bread		
Programme element: **Rhythm song**	Resources: **Drums / voices**	Additional Activities/Actions
Use of combination of different tech elements: **Bass and tone, drum and clap**	Tech played like this: I would like banana bread **Boom** clap **boom** clap	Layering Rhythms This sounds great with the group divided in half, one half playing banana bread and the other
Spoken rhythm sentences, steady rhythm	All one side 2 hands 2 hands (tone) Middle middle	banana bread and the other playing fish and chips!
I would like banana bread **Boom** clap boom clap I would like banana bread **Bing** bang bong	I would like banana bread **Bing** **bang** **bong** All one side 2 hands clap 2 hands (tone) Middle middle	Try your own ground rhythm tunes to put with it.
I would like banana bread **Boom** clap boom clap I would like banana bread **Bing** bang bong HEY!		Play as a round. For a challenge, try as a round with 2nd group starting at the end of the first 'I would like banana bread.'

Level 4

			Strand
Level: 4	Programme element:	Resources:	
	6 / 8 Brain Freeze		
	Tech / dynamics	**Drums**	
Description	**Develop hand placement and introduce 6/8 rhythmical feel**		
	Step 1 Demonstrate hand pattern (alternate hands)		
	Middle side side (stop) (Bass tone tone)		
	M S S (stop) M S S (stop) etc. until established.		
	Left or right hand can be specified to start, but not essential.		
	Continue pattern		
	Step 2 Repeat pattern with opposite hand starting in the middle.		
	M S S (stop) M S S (stop) etc		
	Step 3 Link the two patterns together.		
	Left Right		
	Step 4 Remove the stops Left side side Right side side Count 1 2 3 4 5 6		

Boom Boom with a Twist		
Level: **4**	Programme element:	Strand
	Intro / starters	Resources: **Drums**	
Description	Revise Boom boom my name	

Generate fun and develop focus and attention

Revise Boom boom my name

Boom boom   Simon   boom boom   Arti

Drum   my name   drum   someone else

Once established, each player chooses a title or name from a given category,

e.g. the name of a fruit. The game continues, but players must remember which fruits

are available to choose from.

Boom boom   apple   boom boom   pomegranate

Drum   (my fruit)   drum   (someone else)

Categories can be chosen for fun value or curriculum consolidation and can be

extended with accompanying sound or actions!

Rhythm Layers

Level: **4**	Programme element:	Resources:	Strand
	Rhythm generation	**Drums / additional percussion**	
Description	**Develop and rehearse holding a rhythm against another**		
	Rehearse an existing rhythm pattern.		
	Identify pulse rhythm.		
	Have half the group play the pulse and the other half hold the rhythm pattern.		
	(Switch teams and repeat).		
	Add a second rhythm pattern using the pulse rhythm as a marker.		
	Once tempo is established for both parts, give the parts to the two different sections of the group and play together.		
	Call attention back to pulse and reinforce with pulse-holding drum if necessary.		

		We've Got Glue	Strand
Level: **4**	Programme element: **Rhythm generation**	Resources: **Drums / additional percussion**	
Description	**Maintain focus on the pulse of a rhythm within complementary rhythms** Identify the pulse (main beat of any rhythm) as the glue that holds us together. Play well-known rhythms and recognise how they all play out over a given pulse. **Maintain a steady pulse** and demonstrate how different rhythm sentences fit across the beat. **Pick a common topic**, e.g. favourite foods, and ask each player to **create a personal rhythm** sentence for their favourite food. Provide a solid pulse as players play out their own rhythms together. Call attention to the pulse if needed to consolidate rhythms.	

121

Lion, Octopus, Panda, Duck: *Song cards*

Frog in a Onesie

Programme element:	Resources:
Rhythm songs	**Drums**

Frog in a Onesie (Schematic)

Frog in a Onesie: Schematic (NB – Play 'frog' & 'in' with same hand)

Part 1

	1	2	3	4	1	2	3	4	
Tone									Rpt
Bass	frog	in a	one	sie	frog	in a	one	sie	

Part 2

	1	2	3	4	1	2	3	4	
Tone									Rpt
Bass	frog		frog			in a	sie		

Part 3

	1	2	3	4	1	2	3	4	
Tone	take it	to the	frog	take it	to the	frog	take it	to the	Rpt
Bass									

Part 3 second phrase

	1	2	3	4	1	2	3	4
Tone	rest	rest	rest	rest	rest	rest	rest	rest
Bass								

Lion, Octopus, Panda, Duck: *Song cards*

	Frog in a Onesie	
Programme element: **Rhythm songs**	Resources: **Drums**	Additional Activities/ Actions
A three-part rhythm song Each part has its own rhythmical challenges. Schematic is available on additional card.	Part 3: (All tone notes. Play one phrase, rest one phrase)	In part 2, a 'swallow like a frog'
Part 1: **Frog in a onesie, frog in a onesie, frog in a onesie**	Take it to the frog, take it to the frog, Take it to the… **rest rest, rest, rest.** *(Part 1 Frog in a onesie, frog in a onesie)*	over the two rests provides a
(Frog & in, one sie played with the same hand B T T)	As shown above, in the rest phrase of part 3 part 1 will add the frog and play …frog in a onesie x 2.	fun element to see players'

Part 2:
 	
    Frog   in   a   one   sie,
     B   T   T   B   T
		frog faces
		and helps
		to keep

(All bass notes. This runs across 2 phases of part 1) **Frog** rest **Frog** rest rest **One sie**		time.

Lion, Octopus, Panda, Duck: *Song cards*

Rhythm in the Street		
Programme element:	Resources:	Additional Activities/Actions
Songs	**Drums / voices**	
Rhythm in the classroom		Add a simple pulse beat to
Rhythm in the street		accompany the chant.
Rhythm in your heartbeat when you're stomping down the street		
		Vary the parameters of the
		chant, tempo, volume or voice
Rhythm in the classroom		characteristics.
Rhythm in the street		(Say it like a…giant)
Rhythm in your heartbeat when		
∨ ∨		Follow the syllable patterns on the
you're stomping down the street		drum to match the vocal rhythm.
		Add a couple of accented beats to
		reinforce the lilt of the rhythm.

124

Lion, Octopus, Panda, Duck: *Song cards*

Programme element: **Rhythm songs**	Resources: **Drums, blocks, shakers**	Additional Activities/Actions
A three-part rhythm song for additional percussion		Once song is established, on the count of 4 the leader holds up an instrument or makes a call '123 shakers.'
Part 1: Drums		The shakers then play their phrase on their own.
We are the drummers and we like to drum		Everyone else then joins back in and rhythm continues until next instrument call and another section gets to solo its part.
Part 2: Blocks		If your group has a good degree of mobility, when the command '1 2 3 shakers' is given, all the shaker players change places in the group.
Blocks blocks listen to the blocks		This will work with blocks too but the drums are more difficult.
Part 3: Shakers		So the drummers' response is to stay where they are, throw their hands in the air and shout together 'We are the drummers and we like to drum.' Before returning to the rhythm.
Slow and steady shakers and we'll win the race		

125

References

Referenced in text:

Hull, Arthur (2006) *Drum Circle Facilitation: Building Community Through Rhythm.* USA: Village Music Circles

Stevens, Christine, MSW, MT-BC (2012) *Music Medicine: The Science and Spirit of Healing Yourself With Sound.* Boulder CO: Sounds True, Inc

Further reading

Boneau, J (2020) *The Rumble Zone: leadership strategies in the rough & tumble of change.* Fresno, CA: Ignite press

Edited by Simon Faulkner (2021) *Drum Circles for Specific Population Groups.* London, Jessica Kingsley Publishers

Andrews, Ted (1992) *Sacred Sounds: magic & healing through words & music.* USA, Llewellyn Publications

Acknowledgements

Since switching career paths from Teacher to Drum Circle Facilitator 14 years ago, I have been privileged to work with many gifted, talented and dedicated people. Many of them are working on a daily basis with small groups of people at grassroots level, providing invaluable care, support and education where it really matters. However, there are a few people who have guided and supported me personally at different stages of this journey and I would like to give them a mention here.

It's probably fair to say that I would not have begun this journey if not for a massive amount of encouragement and initial on-the-job training from Tim Scarborough of Rhythmicity. It was Tim who gave me the confidence to embark on this completely new career and also introduced me to Arthur Hull of Village Music Circles. This resulted in me attending Arthur's first UK Playshop training. Arthur's vision and training protocols were a revelation, and the work done at that training has stood me in good stead in the intervening years.

Another person who featured large in these early years – and many times since – is Yvonne Clark, whose extensive practical workshop experience she grafted into me (although I was a quick learner: my job, 'Get there first, put the chairs out, find the tea!'). I will always be grateful to these three – Tim, Arthur and Yvonne – for helping me lay the foundations for all that Talking Rhythms has become.

In writing this manual, there are some specific people who deserve a mention and a thank you. Firstly, to all the staff and pupils who have attended our sessions and who have brought with them their uniqueness, spirit and fun. Particular thanks must go to the staff who have been an amazing support over the years and who are outstandingly dedicated to the young people in their care.

Thanks must also go to Jane Bentley of Art Beat for taking the time to look at an early draft and recommend that I continue writing. Closer to home, there have been a number of close friends who have been a constant source of encouragement and, without whom, I think I would have given up writing very early on. To Derek and Mark, for early proofreading and advice on style and content, Jo and Ali for helping me to silence my inner critic and keep at it throughout all the stages of the writing process, and Kelly for being able to decipher my handwriting and type up, and carry out an initial proofread. Also to Jen at Fuzzy Flamingo for her meticulous, friendly and practical help and advice at the production stage.

Finally, thank you to my wife, Helen, who has put up with a house, garage and trailer full of drums and assorted percussion equipment for the past fourteen years. Whilst

I have been writing this manual, she has listened to and quietly ignored all my doubts and has diligently gone through the text with me to make sure it's understandable before sending for proofreading.

To all of you, '**I thank you!**'

Printed in Great Britain
by Amazon